Democracy and Its Enemies

Political Theory for Today

Series Editor: Richard Avramenko, University of Wisconsin, Madison

Political Theory for Today seeks to bring the history of political thought out of the jargon-filled world of the academy into the everyday world of social and political life. The series brings the wisdom of texts and the tradition of political philosophy to bear on salient issues of our time, especially issues pertaining to human freedom and responsibility, the relationship between individuals and the state, the moral implications of public policy, health and human flourishing, public and private virtues, and more. Great thinkers of the past have thought deeply about the human condition and their situations—books in Political Theory for Today build on that insight.

Titles Published

Tradition v. Rationalism: Voegelin, Oakeshott, Hayek, and Others, by Gene Callahan and Lee Trepanier
Democracy and Its Enemies: The American Struggle for the Enlightenment, by Paul N. Goldstene

Democracy and Its Enemies

The American Struggle for the Enlightenment

Paul N. Goldstene

LEXINGTON BOOKS
Lanham • Boulder • New York • London

Published by Lexington Books
An imprint of The Rowman & Littlefield Publishing Group, Inc.
4501 Forbes Boulevard, Suite 200, Lanham, Maryland 20706
www.rowman.com

Unit A, Whitacre Mews, 26-34 Stannary Street, London SE11 4AB

British Library Cataloguing in Publication Information Available

Library of Congress Cataloging-in-Publication Data

Names: Goldstene, Paul N., 1930- author.
Title: Democracy and its enemies : the American struggle for the Enlightenment / Paul N. Goldstene.
Description: Lanham, Maryland : Lexington Books, [2018] | Series: Political theory for today |
    Includes bibliographical references and index.
Identifiers: LCCN 2018031418 (print) | LCCN 2018039016 (ebook) | ISBN 9781498581752 (Elec-
    tronic) | ISBN 9781498581745 (cloth : alk. paper)
Subjects: LCSH: Democracy--United States. | Power (Social sciences)--Political aspects--United
    States. | Political culture--United States. | Enlightenment--United States.
Classification: LCC JK1726 (ebook) | LCC JK1726 .G646 2018 (print) | DDC 320.973--dc23
LC record available at https://lccn.loc.gov/2018031418

Printed in the United States of America

To my family

Contents

Acknowledgments

The road to a short book is long. That, at least, is my experience. Along the way several people read and offered comments about parts of the manuscript which often became chapters. Accordingly, I appreciated the efforts of Ronald T. Fox, William P. Head, Catherine Hatzakos, Stephen E. Johnson, and Romain Nelsen. Some, such as Isaac Kramnick, Rick Tilman, and Neal Turner, read the entire manuscript at different stages of its development. Others, including Gilbert M. Frimet and Christian S. Larsen, were forthcoming in their willingness to seriously discuss what I was trying to accomplish, while Arc Indexing Inc., Richard Avramenko, Amber Foreman, Ramona June Grey, Madhu Koduvalli, A. Ricardo López-Pedreros, Naomi Minkoff, Joseph C. Parry, Bryndee Ryan, and Lee Trepanier were instrumental to the actuality of this work reaching print. Michael F. Singman read the manuscript more than once, and our subsequent discussions about the centrality of the Enlightenment to what I was trying to say became fundamental. All, whether or not they knew it, were encouraging and helpful, frequently at times where these were most crucial.

Early versions of this effort were typed by Tawn-Marie Gauthey, who was able to discover legible prose within my scribbling, and by Jean Crew at a later point. For quite a while now, Dottie Moore Paige has been indispensable, typing a variety of drafts, tracking down needed information, and otherwise holding my hand during the seemingly endless process of writing and rewriting. Thanks also to William Ludholz and David F. Paige for solving a variety of problems when the computer appeared to go out of control.

My obligations to my immediate family are plain. The consistent, or, actually, insistent, support of my wife Pat, who read and commented on the entire manuscript and had much to do with the cover design, my children, James, Claire, who also read the manuscript and offered some excellent editorial suggestions, Beth, who also helped with the cover design, as well as Jami and Lily, needs not only to be stated, but affirmed here.

Introduction

The Competition of Ideas in America

All cultures, and the political orders they produce, are grounded in a universal human need to confront the material realities of existence. Still, a great variety of configurations evolve from this common imperative. Such diversity manifests a range of physical conditions, along with an impressive plurality of human responses to these conditions. These lead to identifiable systems, as well as to those perceptions, values, and attitudes which coalesce into the myths and ideologies that justify them, and that fuse into a prevailing consciousness and a governing language that tenaciously resist any fundamental criticisms of the economic arrangements which they ultimately reflect. Hence it is the material imperative which is causal to the enormous influence of tradition—inducing those habits of mind and behavior which, as William James points out, literally hold societies together, and any systemic change invariably first occurs at this level.

But, despite the troubled history of the term, it is ideology that directly motivates behavior because it expresses the cultural choices people have made within the strictures of the material realities they confront. Indeed, to deny the indispensable role of ideological agreements is to deprive political inquiry of an essential conception that addresses the issue of how political orders gain the support of a large proportion of a population and, consequently, how to distinguish movements that are truly revolutionary progressive, or even, from those that are not. More immediately, it is to transform a particular ideology into an a priori and unchallengeable truth.

Ideologies are normative. They flow from political doctrines, which are worked out arguments about what should or should not be or, rather inescapably, both, and an ideology emerges when a particular doctrine has attained

1

wide acceptance. However, the broader this acceptance the vaguer the doctrinal roots of an ideology become—allowing vociferous debate about their precise stipulations, but only on the edges, never at the center. Some refer to this center as the core values of a society. Hegel portrays it as the prevailing *Volksgeist*, others as the worldview or consciousness of a population although, unlike core values and ideology itself, these terms carry with them more than the normative content of the doctrine upon which they are predicated. They also incorporate systemically controlling perceptions about what supposedly exists.

While a theory of politics must inquire into the realities of who rules, and why, and how, a doctrine of politics addresses the perhaps more perennial questions of who should rule, and why, and how. Accordingly, it must deal with the issue of how political authority ought to be distributed and, regardless of the vocabulary of the moment, it is in these terms that the notion of a spectrum of "Right," "Center," and "Left" can be most usefully understood. In the modern era, this spectrum is most crucially infused by the Enlightenment. And if, since the Enlightenment, conservatism is to the right and democracy to the left, the liberal idea of rule through a configuration of competing commercial elites is not merely the doctrinal center; it is plainly the dominant ideology of those systems which the Enlightenment has so far produced.

* * *

Thus, for instance, liberal doctrine deeply infuses the controlling ideology of the American population. Its formulations become translated into a language of civic discourse which distrusts the authority of the one, the few, and the many while applauding natural rights and that pluralistic constellation of contending propertied interests which eventuates in rule by competing wealthy elites. Indeed, the degree to which the majority in America, sufficiently absorbed into a liberal culture, accepts this depiction of its own political capacities induces a situation wherein majorities do not trust majorities to govern, even while they have no real confidence in anyone else. But such a "democratic" liberalism is not simply an example of Orwellian doublethink.[1] What it more tellingly discloses are certain of the contradictions that permeate the presiding culture of a nation that emerges from the Enlightenment—a philosophical movement which rapidly becomes an enormous expression of the force of science working itself out in the world.

NOTE

1. George Orwell, *1984: A Novel*, with an Afterword by Erich Fromm, rev. and updated bibliography, A Signet Classic (New York: New American Library, 1981), p. 10 and passim, italicized in first two usages, two words in second usage.

Chapter One

Liberal Economics as a System of Power

The Enlightenment can be viewed as beginning in Western Europe around the middle of the seventeenth century with people such as Thomas Hobbes and ending with American writers like Thomas Jefferson in the early nineteenth century. This is an era wherein the names of Condorcet, Voltaire, and Montesquieu loom large on the continent; Newton and Adam Smith in England and Scotland; Franklin, Paine, and Adams in what will become the United States. But, getting beyond historical categories to the realities of culture and ideology, the Age of Reason has set the terms of debate in the Western world for the past three centuries. It continues to do so. Indeed, its central insistence on the positive possibilities of human beings, as opposed to the dour certainties of tradition, pervade what is known as modernity and the power struggles that define it.

* * *

Whatever their differences about political equality and the human possibilities, those who employ the language of rule in America typically express a common theme. Consciously or not, this is rooted in the premise that the laws of nature are rational, moral, harmonious, consistent, forever and, crucially, the a priori and essential forces that govern the universe. Such are forces that fully incorporate reason, morality, and truth, all of which cohere because each is also the others and, in combination, are the substance of which the natural laws are composed.

Herein reside the eternal verities of the Enlightenment, subject to discovery through the right reason that the natural laws themselves have instilled within the human mind. This involves far more than the instrumental reason that many animals apparently possess. Instead, it demands a quest for the very meaning of reason—a search for those regularities against which truth and the ethical content of human behavior must be measured, and which thereby establish the standard of rationality itself. In its early formulation this was a matter of reason qua reason, of reason alone. But by means of its subsequent association with the empirical approach to evidence, the Enlightenment begins to gather enormous revolutionary power.

Inspired by the newly discovered mechanistic laws of the universe propounded by Isaac Newton, it is from these presuppositions and assumptions that the central dictum of the Enlightenment of rational means to rational ends emerges. And it is from this that the United States is born—its guiding ideas comprising a major consequence of rationalist philosophy. Such is what Henry Steele Commager labeled "the empire of reason,"[1] that which, in America, finds its preeminent political articulation in the ideology of liberalism, a result of a cultural perspective that is saturated not only in the idea of natural law, but also in subsequent claims about natural rights as pivotal derivations of these laws. At bottom, this is because rights are necessary to the search for the laws of nature which instilled these rights into human beings in the first place. Indeed, even when later liberals begin to claim that rights are not really natural but conventional, or socially constructed, the centrality of rights as a moral imperative remains the same.

Yet it is important to note that liberal doctrine also insists that the ability to enjoy these rights depends on the creation of a more rational world: a world which can only be predicated upon the understanding that any attempt to discern the laws that govern the universe through the application of human reason is always in conflict with the dark side of the personality. This is the domain of the passions—those elements of antireason that exist within everyone and which incessantly work against a progressively improving comprehension of the rational and virtuous consistencies of nature. Such are appetites that know no bounds, disposing all human beings toward factional tyranny and inevitably rendering any instance of political authority dangerous to rights—and which, as Sheldon Wolin notes, assures that liberalism has always represented "a philosophy of sobriety . . . and disenchantment."[2] Beyond this, while reason, passions, and rights are intrinsic to human nature, and while rights are equal and the passions may well be, the talent to employ reason in the service of rights and, invariably, of the passions as well, is genetically unequal among people—a conviction that must oppose democracy and which profoundly informs the entirety of the liberal tradition.

It is precisely these propositions about the human psyche that move the early liberals toward a trifurcation of societal existence into a public sphere of government and the private spheres of economics and the personal: a view that is soon simplified by subsuming the personal within the economic. The dual results of this outlook are modern constitutional government and capitalism, each of which derives from a doctrinal insistence on a competition among the more rational of human beings that might curtail the inclinations of the passions within categorically distinct realms of human activity. It is a formulation of reality that yields the political and the economic as two separate and pluralistic orders which demand distinct systems of competing elites that check themselves even as they constrain each other.

* * *

All of this is predicated upon the idea of the sovereignty of the people as a central manifestation of the Enlightenment. The human experience is replete with political orders which are rooted in the argument that the authority of the state expresses, and can be rightly constrained, only by a will that is not of this world. Yet, as a refrain that accompanies their long crawl away from mysticism and toward a more scientific approach to the problems of evidence, people slowly come to insist that such limitations on authority should be grounded in more observable and, perhaps, more mundane realities. This is a notion that begins to attain systemic effect with the gathering of the forces of revolution in those areas of Europe touched by the Enlightenment, emanating as a conception which gradually becomes known as popular sovereignty—a conception that steadily grows in influence throughout much of the planet. As a result, for an increasing array of systems in the modern era, if a doctrine of politics is to receive a serious hearing, it must somehow assert that its foundation expresses the will of the people; a formulation about the source of political authority which includes every person within a given jurisdiction in an equal manner; a unified entity that resides in this world and prior to any government. Whether or not human beings are equal in their rational capacities, they are equal enough for this.

It follows that the state, that is, the legal sovereign—that which, for instance, is the object of recognition in international relations—whatever its substance and details, can only be created when authority is delegated into it by the political sovereign, now the people—all the people equally, not merely certain categories of people—and, because the political sovereign, by definition, cannot divest itself of its own sovereignty, the authority so delegated is always considered to be merely on loan to the state. Furthermore, these delegations may be adjusted or even abolished by the will of the people. That is, a state remains a state only as long as the people continues to consent to its existence by continuing to support the authority allocations that initially established it and which thereafter work to maintain it.

Propelled by the liberal idea of natural rights, these abstractions are transformed into a salient social fiction, and the sovereign people emerges as essential to the issue of legitimacy and, it follows, who is entitled to rule. In brief, a government not predicated upon the consent of the governed is not really a government.

It is on this basis that the idea of the social contract associated with John Locke emerges, its advent representing a supreme act of human reason. The agreement of each with all among the human beings who populate the earth—or, as is more likely, a particular part of the earth—is to leave a state of nature and form a society, or what might be viewed as the pact of union. To then further agree to create a civil society, that is, a society with a government, constitutes what is generally understood as the social contract. It is this which establishes a configuration of political authority which is limited to the protection and promotion of natural rights as these are enunciated by an agreement which expresses the will of the people that, by allegedly consenting to this agreement, has been implicitly transformed into the sovereign people.[3] With these constraints on the state, as Thomas Paine will put it, man is born anew—history is expunged—and the human world begins again.

* * *

Such abstractions are at the core of the liberal vision of reality, a vision which is often accompanied by the assertion that people are not forever burdened by an inherent nature; that what they are inextricably is a tabula rasa; a blank slate. Unlike other doctrinal contentions, wherein the varying qualities of human beings are conclusively fixed and their possibilities fully expressed, here there are no historical and, accordingly, no cultural restrictions on the rational possibilities of the species.

But, not quite. Actually, liberals have always expounded a very definite view of human nature, one which precedes the contract and, in fact, is literally released by it. And within this view lurks certain assumptions about the substance of the human psyche and progress which are well labeled by C. B. Macpherson as "possessive individualism":[4] a formulation which proclaims that people are born whole and acquisitive, and that nothing of what they truly are is a result of the environment in which they happen to exist. What historically ramifies from this is the rational economic man of capitalism—an expression of those natural laws that are anterior to human history, and which any contract predicated upon reason must respect.

Clearly, the weight placed on the political and the economic is not the same. What emanates is a public sector, conceived of as the state, a necessary but inferior realm which must be artificially constructed by the careful design of human beings if liberty is to be maintained and if the tyranny that must ensue if a single faction gains total authority is to be avoided. Simultaneously released is a private sector of economics which is natural and, therein, closer to the reason, morality, and truth of the laws of nature. Such is an arena epitomized by competing entrepreneurs who automatically restrain each other and whose productive behavior and resulting financial position will demonstrate their relative rational worth to humanity. This is the sphere of the free market—a sphere that emerges from the inherent human passion for material gain and wherein the level of personal accumulation is indicative of the inborn differences in rational talent.

* * *

Leading to American exceptionalism and its financial version of equal opportunity, this is an ideological position grounded in what comes to be known as the labor theory of value. Here economic wealth is defined as useful goods and services, as opposed to, for instance, gold, or some other standard. Beyond this, wealth is considered to be produced by the application of human labor to natural resources, to which no one has an automatic claim. Such is the theory. The doctrinal inference must be that people are entitled to the exact amount of wealth they earn, that is, labor to produce.

To store up wealth in the form of money is no problem for the labor theory. But to then use money to acquire more money, in short, to attain that which is referred to as profit, is to violate the distributive demands that logically emanate from the theory itself. This is because money represents labor already expended and paid for, and to use money to make money is to assert ownership of wealth that had to be produced by the labor of others who, to the extent of the claim, did not receive the wealth to which they were entitled. Thus, according to the labor theory of value, profit is theft or, as some prefer, unearned increment. Yet, as the liberal perspective develops, profit becomes habitually perceived as a derivation of the property right and, to this point, has increasingly crowded out the labor theory in the vocabulary and discourse of liberal systems.

Those who substantially achieve on these terms will be the few or, perhaps, more than a few, who have developed their superior capacity for reason into the operational reality of a superior rational ability—and who, by getting rich, or even relatively rich, have inadvertently helped to alleviate a perennial economic scarcity through their contributions to a greater material production. This is defined as progress, and it is this for which they are being monetarily rewarded. In this manner, reason is expressed as success within an entrepreneurial system of price competitors. Hence it is only reasonable to think that the private sphere will reveal those who are sufficiently rational to govern the political sphere, and who must govern if there is any possibility of natural rights being accurately comprehended and protected by the state, and of finding their legal expression in civil rights and civil liberties.

Nevertheless, while the natural tendency of a proper allocation of personal wealth is a general increase in usable goods and services, the natural tendency of government is to become a tyranny which will destroy those rights which are vital to free markets. Engagement in the public realm is always greeted with suspicion. It is certainly not an activity that liberals admire. Contrary to the democratic perspective, to be involved in politics is never portrayed as a positive employment of the true self, or even as a disreputable vehicle through which to enhance the development of one's more desirable qualities. This is best left to the private realm, an arena which automatically demonstrates who the most deserving people are.

* * *

What follows is a liberal position that argues for a pluralistic order which historically results from the transformation of private wealth into a stratum of rule by competing propertied elites. To identify such leaders all that need be done is to look at their bank accounts, since it is these which announce the level of success attained within a realm of equal opportunity—that is, the opportunity to acquire money as the signification of merit and worth in compliance with the abiding realities of commodity man.

It becomes self-evident that the most noble disposition of the species is—and always will be—economic, and that technological and monetary progress is what human existence should be about. In fact, an increase in material wealth, both systemic and personal, is the only notion of progress that liberalism can really entertain, and that the most rational few ought to rule simply reflects a reluctant understanding that government is required if the anarchy of a state of nature, and a resulting diminution of the enjoyment of rights, is not to prevail.

But this has to be buttressed by the proper form of government, and here the laws of nature must instruct the contract. A natural and automatic competition among entrepreneurs—as this is propelled by consumer sovereignty and the consequent vagaries of supply and demand—needs to be rationally replicated in the public realm. Given the tyrannical tendencies of human beings, this must follow the republican principle, whereby authority is delegated in such a manner that it is vested in the various offices of government, and not in those who may happen to be filling these offices, while the holder of an office is viewed as separable from the office and merely cloaked with its authority for only as long as they occupy it for a specified term. Thus the office itself is authorized and, thereby, immune from the law because, by definition, authority cannot be charged, indicted, prosecuted or, for that matter, sued unless those cloaked with the authority agree. However, the holder of the office is always conceived of as a private individual and is not so protected, even while in office.

In further compliance with the republican formulation, those who constitute such a state should not do so more than briefly if they are to escape being corrupted by the lure of public power which will invariably whet the natural appetite for tyranny. Then, having dirtied themselves for a time in the public realm of politics, members of the ruling elites should return to the cleansing principles of the private realm of economics, leaving to others of their financial station the obligation to exercise political authority for a similarly short duration.

* * *

Plainly, the timeless purpose of the social contract, as this is manifested in free markets and constitutional government, is to translate and clarify the rights of the people and protect them through the state—most crucially the right to productive property and, in more sophisticated versions, the rights of property itself—as these are demarcated as a region of liberty into which, by definition, even a minimal state cannot intrude. The liberals who wrote the United States Constitution more than agreed with this. However, they were also certain that human passions guaranteed that all governments are fundamentally disposed to tyranny; whether these are in the hands of the one, the few, or the many; whether they are executive, judicial, or legislative in form; or monarchical, aristocratic, or democratic in principle—forms and principles which, because of the nature of man, would soon degenerate into rule by a dictatorship, an oligarchy, or a mob.[5] Above all, the probable tyranny of the many had to be prevented or, at least, mitigated, since it was clear that, among these tyrannies, majority government was the most dangerous to liberty because the simple arithmetic of the matter places so many tyrants in authority. Sharing a fear that majority rule will introduce a regime of mediocrity which will crush individual rights, those in Philadelphia patently rejected democracy. Instead, they devised an order wherein the authority of the larger number is foreclosed and within which the countervailing disputes among the few who hold substantial productive property, and whose reason is less susceptible to sabotage by the passions than that of most people, will control the functional realities of the state.

Yet, while it is only rational that a few are most qualified to rule, the assumptions that justify the liberal order always insist that even the best people cannot be trusted with political authority and, indisputably, not for too long. It is hardly surprising that, throughout the history of liberalism, the tension between the free market and the state is endemic, and that the emphasis is on the positive domain of economics which will rationally and productively proceed according to the true principles that naturally regulate this domain if not interfered with by government. Certainly, it is only this which allows the material deprivation that has characterized human existence to be alleviated through the unrestrained workings of the perfect competition that epitomizes a free market. And it is only this version of economics which might assure that the rights of life and liberty will be publicly clarified and hopefully guaranteed.

If laissez-faire is not ideal, it is the best that the propensities of human nature will allow. Material scarcity can never be eliminated because of the insatiable passion for wealth that is natural to everyone—a passion that is always functioning at the highest level of intensity. Or, simply put, in the matters of production and distribution, enough can never be enough because the very idea of economic sufficiency cannot ever be in harmony with those avaricious proclivities of human beings which transform material scarcity into a permanent condition of the species.

* * *

Beyond all else, liberalism is a paean to those economic truths presumably embedded in the universal laws of nature. These are at the foundation of what James Madison considered a semi-rational competition of interests as opposed to the irrational politics of social-class struggle.[6] Since the late-seventeenth century it is an outlook which, to the liberal mind, relies on the melding of reason and empiricism into natural philosophy—a combination that acclaims the efficacy of capitalist economics and those impressive technological achievements that will eventuate in the industrial revolution and the enormous increase in the available wealth which comprises the foundation of what is often referred to as the modern world.

Tempered by dynamic equilibriums within and between both market and state, the private pursuit of wealth becomes the presiding liberal expression of the Enlightenment. It follows that the legal possession of property provides empirical evidence of that meritorious behavior which, when properly educated, finally comprises the tangible actualization of a naturally superior rational capacity and its development into a rational ability. This is a claim that infuses the liberal notion of individualism. Accordingly, the only legitimate purpose of the civic realm is to articulate and ensure the rights that attend a very private being whose essential self is prior to culture, society, and politics—an individualism that conclusively represents humanity's best chance to mitigate the incessant pressures of economic scarcity and the threat of political despotism.

This idea of individualism is at the core of the liberal commitment to a system of equal opportunity wherein people are free to seize an equal chance to financially demonstrate how unequal they really are.[7] Hence human beings, who are simultaneously rational and irrational to varying degrees, are to struggle with this central contradiction within their own personalities through that pecuniary activity which determines their relative success or failure in the capitalist market. That the goal of individualism and equal opportunity is to identify the superior rational abilities of the few who make the greatest contributions to material production and the economic accumulation of society is only natural in the liberal worldview. Not only do some people deserve a greater command on wealth than others. It is also rational to contend that the rich are the most qualified to rule in the name of the general welfare. Indeed, this is sufficiently self-evident to be hardly worthy of mention.

* * *

Such an outlook has led to an implicit agreement in America that major ideological conflicts are now exhausted because they have been resolved by a liberal configuration that the rest of the globe should rationally be encouraged to emulate. The resulting contention that ideology is effectively archaic also locks into place the supposed good sense of majorities in the United States, often proposing that the nation is inhabited by a practical people who rightly look to others to govern and who overtly or, at least, implicitly, accept the assertion of Karl R. Popper—among numerous others—that anyone who holds an "ideological" position must be instilled with a touch of madness, which is then associated with an undesirable extremism or, even worse, fanaticism. In the 1950s this view became articulated as "the end of ideology"[8]—a theoretical penchant which declared that an essentially consistent equilibrium and notably, thereby, an absence of class conflict, had come to exemplify the more "advanced" areas of the globe. All that remained was to apply the insights of structural functionalism, or "systems analysis," by tinkering with the details within the accepted parameters of the established order, making minor adjustments in regard to policy outcomes: an affirmation which is more recently voiced in the pronouncement that the United States represents both the purpose and "the end of history."[9]

It is within this context that Louis Hartz can propose that America is a monolithically liberal nation because the social, economic, and political doctrines enunciated by Locke are so deeply engrained within its political culture that nothing else can be effectively visualized—for this country or for the world—a situation within which all occasions of ideological dispute become insignificant.[10] But, in this variation on "consensus history," it should be noted that Hartz never asserts that ideology has ended. On the contrary, his point is that one ideology has attained such supremacy in the United States that other ideological formulations cannot be seriously entertained, or even comprehended.

However, if for Hartz it is the ideology of liberalism that grounds and stabilizes an America that—outside of, to some extent, parts of the South—is purportedly devoid of the aristocratic and monarchical remnants of an earlier European history, for others it is the ideology of democracy that comprises the dominant theme of the American cultural experience. In this rendition too, ideological conflict is found only on the extremes and is operationally trivial—coming either from disillusioned malcontents suffused with the alien ideas of a European socialism; or from the adherents of an equally European conservatism which is historically antirational and antiempirical at its base; a philosophical Romanticism that accepts no limits on the political authority that should appropriately flow to those who are felt to be the qualified few.

The evidence abundantly indicates that Hartz is correct; that since before the consolidation of the country into a nation-state through the catalyst of the Civil War; indeed, prior to the writing of the Constitution itself; the premier

American agreements are most accurately understood as manifestations of the Lockean social contract, an idea which begins to generally emerge in the England of the seventeenth century. Here the authority to govern is to be shared by those who populate an elite structure of rival entrepreneurs—those who best perceive the immutable laws of nature as made apparent by their business fortunes and the natural laws of economics. If Locke would cede to the monarch prerogative control over foreign affairs, a jurisdiction which involves populations not party to the contract and whose rights are not protected by it, this does not quite become the American formulation, wherein the authority of the executive is checked by the authority of opposing departments within the central government, and which are themselves restrained by the executive, as well as by a multiplicity of other sovereign governments known as states. Thus the will of the sovereign people of the United States is divided from the will of the sovereign people of the various states, leading to the notions of dual sovereignty and dual citizenship.

Such is a configuration that might discourage tyranny, and wherein those whose superior rational qualifications are made plain by their personal material holdings are thereby to compete within the public realm in a way that encourages the formulation and implementation of public policy through a pluralistic working out of their differences at an elite level of engagement. This should, at least, induce an approximation of right rule which, in the liberal pantheon, is as near to it as the human disposition will permit.

In this fashion the mainstream of the Enlightenment elevates economics over the classical and supposedly arcane idea of the polis which, no longer perceived as a noble calling, rapidly comes to be portrayed as an inferior arena of human activity. The doctrine of the free market accordingly attains an intellectual pedigree that complies with the newly discovered fact of natural philosophy that human behavior is endlessly driven by an avarice that expresses an unremitting passion for pecuniary gain. What results is a commercial elitism which is always implicit in the Lockean contention that liberty depends on an atomization of public power through an appropriate social contract—a profoundly progressive stance at the time of its inception because it substantially expanded the number of people thought to be meritorious enough to wield political authority.

* * *

All of this induces a habit of mind which insists that the essence of the species is not changeable; that it is doggedly and naturally fixed in its overweening appetite for lucre; that no real solutions are to be found within the public realm; and that an equal opportunity to get rich leads to the identification of those most qualified to govern. Any objection to these realities is tenaciously resisted by the bedrock of a liberal ideology which, in America, except for spasmodic egalitarian periods, yields what is basically a static system, and wherein the democratic conception of the polis as a positive influence for human development is dismissed as radical or little more than idealistic nonsense. Hence, beyond the further accumulation of material wealth, there can be no true improvement in the human condition—an aspiration which is rendered beyond the pale because of what is, innately, an economic personality.

That people of property should be in charge is nothing less than rational. In any event, the obligations of the capitalist state are minimal, the major one being to legally enforce agreements freely entered into in a price-competitive market while not allowing government, which is man-made, or conventional, to otherwise intervene into the sphere of economics which is natural and, therefore, preferable. Even the British reform liberals, such as John Stuart Mill and John Maynard Keynes, who contend that a Newtonian balance is not an automatic result of the market, and that incomes have to be adjusted by governmental intervention into the sector of distribution, agree with this when it comes to the sector of production. Thus what is now referred to as the welfare state, or the warfare state or, more cogently, the intertwining of both, in no sense challenges the bedrock premises of liberalism about human nature, the meaning of opportunity, merit, and progress and, as a consequence, how the contours and content of the public interest are to be determined. This is to be expected. As the dominant expression of the Enlightenment, a liberal culture is always more about a rational elitism than democracy and, accordingly, more about economics than politics.

NOTES

1. Henry Steele Commager, *The Empire of Reason: How Europe Imagined and America Realized the Enlightenment* (Garden City, NY: Anchor Press, Double Day, Anchor Books, 1978).

2. Sheldon S. Wolin, *Politics and Vision: Continuity and Innovation in Western Political Thought* (Boston: Little Brown and Co., 1960), pp. 29–24.

3. Cf., "The Second Treatise of Civil Government," in John Locke, *Two Treatises of Government*, with a supplement, *Patriarcha* by Robert Filmer, ed. with an intro. by Thomas I. Cook, The Hafner Library of Classics, no. 2, ed. by Oskar Piest (New York: Hafner Publishing Co., 1947), in particular, chap. 1, "Of the Beginning of Political Societies," pp. 16–13 and passim.

4. C.B. Macpherson, *The Political Theory of Possessive Individualism: Hobbes to Locke* (Oxford, England: Oxford University Press, Oxford University Paperback, 1964), p. v and passim, quoted for emphasis in the original in its first usage. This is derived from "the original seventeenth-century individualism" which propounds a "conception of the individual as essentially the proprietor of his own person or capacities, owing nothing to society for them," and wherein "the individual was seen neither as a moral whole, nor as part of a larger social whole, but as an owner of himself," ibid., p. 3.

5. Cf., James Madison, "The Federalist," in Alexander Hamilton, John Jay, and James Madison, *The Federalist: A Commentary on the Constitution of the United States: Being a Collection of Essays Written in Support of the Constitution Agreed Upon September 17, 1787, by the Federal Convention*, no. 41, with an intro. by Edward Mead Earle, The Modern Library (New York: Random House, n.d.), p. 313.

6. Ibid., in particular, no. 10, pp. 53–62.

7. For empirical verification of this point, see W. Lloyd Warner, with the collaboration of Wilfrid C. Bailey, Arch Cooper, Walter Eaton, A. B. Hollingshead, Carson McGuire, Marchia Meeker, Bernie Neugarten, Joseph Rosenstein, Evon Z. Vogt Jr., and Donald Wray, *Democracy in Jonesville: A Study in Quality and Inequality*, The Academy Library (New York: Harper and Row, Publishers, Harper Torchbooks, 1949), especially chap. 2, "Status in the Democracy of Jonesville," pp. 22–34. A fuller development of such evidence is found in W. Lloyd Warner and Paul S. Lunt, *The Social Life of a Modern Community*, in W. Lloyd Warner, Yankee City Series, 6 vols. (New Haven: Yale University Press, 1941), vol. 1. Also see Robert S. Lynd and Helen Merrell Lynd, *Middletown: A Study in Contemporary American Culture* (New York: Harcourt, Brace and Co., 1929); *Middletown in Transition: A Study in Cultural Conflicts* (New York: Harcourt, Brace and Co., 1937); and Daniel Bell, "The Background and Development of Marxian Socialism in the United States," in *Socialism and American Life*, ed. by Drew Egbert and Stow Persons, 11 vols., Princeton Studies in American Civilization (Princeton, NJ: Princeton University Press, 1952), vol. 1, pp. 213–405.

8. Daniel Bell, *The End of Ideology: On the Exhaustion of Political Ideas in the Fifties*, rev. ed. (Cambridge: Harvard University Press, 2000), especially, "The End of Ideology in the West: An Epilogue," pp. 393–408 and "Afterword, 1988: The End of Ideology Revisited," pp. 409–47.

9. The academic popularity, especially among liberals, of Francis Fukuyama, *The End of History and the Last Man* (New York: The Free Press, 1992), is instructive. Also see Francis Fukuyama, "The End of History?," *The National Interest*, Summer 1989, pp. 3–18. Cf., the development of the classical Greek idea of "*thymos*" as the major theme in Fukuyama, *End of History*, p. xvi and passim, a need which inspires human beings to "seek recognition of their own worth, or of the people, things, or principles that they invest with worth," ibid., p. xvii. As employed therein, however, this motivation typifies only "certain human beings" who will, ideally, strive for the "things" of material wealth in the contemporary world, wherein the dangers of war have rendered a military expression of unequal attainment no longer rational, ibid., p. xxiii, and, especially, Part V, "The Last Man," pp. 283–339. Paralleling earlier contentions about "the end of ideology," such an argument is useful for understanding this element within the liberal perspective. In this regard, the conception of *thymos* is also notably similar to the assumptions about human passions and appetites that invariably infuse the doctrine of capitalism, cf., for instance, John Adams, "Discourses on Davila," in *The Works of John Adams: Second President of the United States*, with a life of the author and notes and illustrations by Charles Francis Adams, 10 vols. (Boston: Charles C. Little and James Brown, 1851), vol. 6, "Works on Government," in particular, p. 232, and, more generally, pp. 232–35 and passim, italicized for emphasis in the original in its first usage.

10. Louis Hartz, *The Liberal Tradition in America: An Interpretation of American Political Thought Since the Revolution* (New York: Harcourt, Brace and World, 1955).

Chapter Two

The Conservative Consequences of Liberal Supremacy

Liberalism is the presiding political expression of the Enlightenment in America. Yet another doctrine emanates from the Age of Reason which also informs the texture of the national experience. This equally insists on a regime of the most rational. Here, however, elite competition is not required because those who are actually capable of being in charge can be trusted to do so. That is, there exist a few whose inborn capacity for reason renders them fully qualified to comprehend the good of all and to govern accordingly.

Such a contention always affirms, directly or indirectly, that once those capable of ruling are identified—invariably through a proclamation of self-evidence by those who have been previously so identified and who are, thereby, qualified to make such a determination—it becomes ridiculous to interfere with them by ceding any authority to people who have either less knowledge, or no knowledge at all, about the true principles of politics. What emerges is a conception of a superbly talented elite which is instilled with a public acumen that it is only irrational to resist—a stratum which should rule unfettered even by the influence of lesser elites; to say nothing of the general run of humanity. Such is a central postulate of conservative thought since Plato and before: that true leaders are available; that who they are will become apparent to those who are already true leaders; and that to constrain the capable by those who, by definition, are less than capable is a logically indefensible stance.

Whether it bases these claims on an innately superior capacity for insight, intuition, will, or even blood intuition, this is the historical foundation of all conservatism. It is a perspective which in America, as distinct from its concurrent European counterpart, is not grounded in a Romantic epistemology and its corollary assertions about the critical importance of sentiment and

feeling to proper rule. On the contrary, in concordance with its liberal com-
patriot, conservatism in the United States flows from a conception of the
rational laws of nature which only can be discovered through the exercise of
reason by a naturally qualified few. Thus, within what might be thought of as
the conservative Enlightenment, the knowledge necessary to right rule is
found in the natural laws; the capacity to comprehend these laws dispropor-
tionately exists among people; and, usually, this self-proclaimed capacity
must be cultivated into ability through a proper education. But this is not
enough. Each of these are propositions which also attend the liberal notion of
leadership. However, for liberals no one can be trusted to wield unchecked
authority, including those who comprise the very elites which presumably
should govern, since the rational faculties of even the best of people are
flawed due to the tyrannical tendencies of their interior passions. In the
conservative portrayal of an ultimate elite, they are not.

Accordingly, within the modern school of European conservatism, of
which Edmund Burke is a founding member, total confidence is to be be-
stowed upon those unique few who possess a superior capacity to feel the
vital truths of the national history. Conversely, for American conservatives in
the tradition, for instance, of Alexander Hamilton and John Marshall, the
crucial criterion for elite membership is found not in feeling, but in right
reason. Yet every conservative is committed to a regime of the appropriate
kind of people—those who can be trusted to rule—a regime wherein it plainly takes one to know one.

But to claim that the special knowledge required to govern can be fully
understood and acted upon by none but an ultimate elite is never popular in a
country that historically represents the liberal revolution of market efficiencies against the concentrated authority of the dynastic governments that once
typified the Western world—and that continue to predominate throughout
most of the globe. Hence, in a nation saturated in a liberal suspicion of
government, the conservative view is rarely articulated out loud. It is far
more typically implied. Nevertheless, the conservative Enlightenment in
America deeply infuses a corporate system that logically emanates from the
capitalist commitments of the liberal Enlightenment.

* * *

It is frequently contended that the United States has now entered a postindustrial era, a condition typically delineated as one of highly sophisticated
technology wherein information, as opposed to the more traditional designa-
tions of land, labor, and capital, emerges as the crucial factor of production.
Or, as Daniel Bell famously put it, for contemporary economics "knowledge
not labor, is the source of value."[1] While knowledge is not information, but
is that which supposedly makes sense of information, the magnifying importance of each is generally attributed to the fact that the provision of services,

as distinguished from the production of goods, has come to characterize economic activity in the Western nations.

As the material basis of the end-of-ideology and the end-of-history perspectives,[2] this is a formulation that has attained substantial currency. Yet it is grounded in questionable perceptions. It should be evident that the discovery, organization, and application of information all involve an expenditure of those kinds of energy which precisely constitute instances of human labor. It is equally evident that goods are almost invariably required for any service to take place and that information is clearly pivotal to the creation of each. In other words, as Bell clearly understood, the arrival of postindustrialism does not eliminate the necessity of labor as a fundamental element of the system.

All of this notwithstanding, the information revolution has arrived, accompanied by an enormous augmentation of economic abundance. This is especially so as the vestiges of the price-competitive markets of capitalism are more blatantly replaced by those technologically inspired corporate entities which actually represent a revolution against capitalism in reference to both the means and mode of production. And, if American business is presently more focused on services than on goods, this is simply because reason dictates that the required manufacturing of both finished and unfinished goods more commonly takes place elsewhere around the globe where workers are cheaper and more pliable, governmental subsidies more available, and environmental protections weaker and easier to avoid.

The real question is the extent to which such a transition toward multinationalism, and the human behavior it demands, causes a significant change in cultural habits and, as a consequence, in the values and attitudes that infuse the manner in which people typically react to the material world. Indeed, for a liberal nation, the central issue becomes whether technological advance is propelling the country toward a situation wherein the possibilities of individual liberty are enhanced or diminished. Or, more specifically, the problem is where the dangers to government by a configuration of competing rational elites are actually coming from—if they really lurk within an expanded diversity of civic power or within a greater conservative concentration of power and authority as a manifestation of modernity itself. For these reasons it is useful to understand a postindustrial order not as a service economy but as a particular arrangement of publicly effective power and of the human relationships which this arrangement requires—along with their reflections in the legalities of political authority through which such power is formally articulated.

* * *

According to the liberal outlook, market power, or an economic monopoly, will be quickly transformed into the unrestrained authority of a plutocracy. But this is very improbable in a truly free market suffused by entrepreneurial struggle and an absence of patent protections. Nevertheless, as Adam Smith would have it, in the rare event an industry proves to be unavoidably monopolistic it should be removed from the private realm of the market and placed within the public realm of the state.[3] Otherwise the tremendous leverage of a monopoly will eradicate market after market by selling below cost until the entire system of price competition—and with it the efficiency and liberty that emanate from those innovations in productive techniques that free markets induce—is destroyed. Hence natural monopolies must be socialized—a point that continues to elude those neoclassical proponents of market values who selectively employ Smith in support of their Social Darwinist musings about the benefits of a voraciously unfettered capitalism.

It is, however, precisely such musings which allow the United States to continue to portray itself as a land of equal opportunity: a formulation of tremendous allure to people who historically inhabit an oppressive world of economic scarcity. Yet, while free markets never really exemplified economic endeavor in America[4]—or anywhere else, for that matter—those particles of it that did exist have now been dissolved into the productive rationality of postindustrial planning which far surpasses in efficiency the rationality of the invisible hand that presumably regulates the workings of an entrepreneurial order. In fact, the development of more sophisticated technology and its application to production, along with its demand for corporate concentrations to organize capital, labor, and planning for the long-range investment of each, rather quickly outstripped the capacity of capitalist systems to endure.

What emerges is the augmented power of the conservative Enlightenment. This is only reasonable. Except under conditions of extreme material privation, unplanned demand seldom dictates supply, and if what economists like to call consumer sovereignty is required for capitalism, then what is dominant cannot be so described. That which can be produced is usually produced. Then a market is devised and finally made operational by stimulating demand through advertising as well as by the spending policies of a variety of governments and governmental agencies. And all this is done in the name of "free enterprise" which is nowhere to be found. Instead, given what John Kenneth Galbraith depicts as "want creation" and "the revised sequence," as well as "the paramount position of production"[5] within the substance of American values, an economy of scale has come to prevail.

Still, what the national flirtation with a capitalist order actually did was what capitalism does best. It generated huge aggregates of venture capital, the holders of which, in compliance with their acculturation into the liberal Enlightenment and its view of human nature and the natural laws of economics, must employ in relentlessly seeking profitable outlets to further augment their own pecuniary position and, it rationally follows, the totality of available wealth.

In other words, whether or not free markets were ever empirically characteristic, the culture of capitalism rewarded behavior that precisely performed the historical function that Karl Marx attributes to capitalism as a system: providing the monetary and technological foundation for an ever-greater efficiency in production. Furthermore, as amply demonstrated in many regions of the planet, any attempt to achieve such efficiency without an a priori and adequate financial base can only eventuate in the abject failure of the economic order unless a substantial infusion of capital from elsewhere can be found. It is this which V. I. Lenin and Leon Trotsky, among others, clearly grasped in respect to the position of the Soviet Union in 1917, and that now drives the major policies of many "emerging economies."

All of which leads to the crucial role of foreign investment, or what is currently known as globalization, a constellation of de facto cartels that rationally accords with an incessant quest for corporate profitability and, more to the point, for higher rates of profit on money invested as well as the size of the enterprise itself. In many parts of the world, this also brings with it an impressive amount of outside control and the invariable intimations of imperialism and, at moments, an earlier age of colonialism. It thus introduces tensions which are caused by the fusion of emerging parochial nationalistic claims with a multicultural perspective that is substantially furthered by the transnational aspirations of corporate enterprise.

But, while this has everything to do with the conservative Enlightenment, capital accumulation, and financial liquidity, it has nothing to do with free markets. As the history of commerce, which long predates any identifiable contention for free markets, amply testifies, a business culture does not depend on the existence of capitalism. What finally makes an order capitalistic is the process through which the prices of goods and services required for production, as well as those which regulate consumption, are established. Prices thereby become a consequence of the ratio between available supply and effective demand as this is determined by the natural randomness of entrepreneurial and consumer behavior. However, within a postindustrial epoch, prices are actually set by the perceived interests of those who are able to manage them and who can incorporate their effects into the projections of their market planning, including what is often referred to as "planned obsolescence."[6] This logically leads to the necessity of ensuring sufficient demand, and advertising and the state become the biggest per-dollar businesses in the system, steadily replacing the spontaneity of the much-vaunted sovereignty of the consumer.

It is important to note that such planning is typically a feature of entire industries and not merely that of discrete firms within a given industry, even though, in matters of pricing, there is usually an industry leader which the others follow. What results is what Thorstein Veblen described as an economic arrangement wherein price competition among sellers is defunct and within which effective price competition only takes place between sellers and buyers.[7] Hence those who run the economy reasonably prefer a situation wherein prices are subject to administration or conventions or, maybe less politely, fixing, to the maximum extent possible as these are instituted by people who wield sufficient market power to do so.

This vitally infuses a business system rooted in the conservative Enlightenment—a system within which firms compete in any way that is purportedly not criminal but, contrary to an incessant barrage of propaganda about entrepreneurialism, rarely demonstrates any semblance of the those price-competitive markets that signify the presence of capitalist activity. Within such an order, prices will predictably reflect the monopoly or monopsony position of one company, or the oligopolistic or agreements of a few in combination and, where market power of this kind is paramount, capitalism is not.

* * *

For a while liberals, who always worry about concentrated power, and some of whom came to realize that antitrust efforts did not work, could find a bit of comfort in the assurance that the productive preeminence of the few was restrained by the competing interests of equally unified suppliers of labor, raw materials, and venture capital, as well as by large purchasers who then retailed the eventual merchandise and services—a view that came to be known as "countervailing power."[8] Yet the ideological desire for ever-greater economic efficiency and, accordingly, enhanced rates of profit did not stabilize in this manner. On the contrary, it proceeded further down the path of financial amalgamation as the supposed loci of countervailing power became engulfed by increasingly fewer corporations—however numerous their divisions—especially by those engaged in what socialists traditionally refer to as the basic industries upon which all other businesses, including those that compose the underground economy, depend.

It is, for example, evident that, where union contracts exist, they are now part of the cost accounting and overall planning of major companies, offering them added predictability about relatively long-range expenditures and income. These same firms coordinate purchasing and prices; they have avidly digested the suppliers of necessary raw materials; and they have largely released themselves from the fluctuations of the money markets by becoming banks that finance not only their own ventures, but which extend investment capital and credit to lesser businesses, as well as loans to the eventual consumers. In addition, they increasingly regulate the retailing and servicing of their own production, either directly, or through the technique of franchising. Much of this is the consequence of buyouts and is, therefore, a matter of legal ownership. Where this is not yet the case, primarily with certain suppliers, subcontractors, law firms, and advertising agencies, the purchasing and loaning leverage of large corporate operations affords them the de facto ability to dictate the details of pricing, supply and, finally, of the product or service they are buying.

* * *

As this process continues, small business becomes the captive of big business and subject to the laws which are written for its benefit. Anything herein that might resemble capitalism prevails only on the fringes of the system, and only for as long as it is tolerated and not driven out by huge companies drying up the flow of revenues, supplies, and information to lesser firms—or by entering the same business and temporarily selling selected items below cost—or by myriad other manipulations that work to further maximize and secure their market power.

It is through the conservative Enlightenment that capitalism is dissolved. What looms in its place is a transnational order of vertical integration, wherein control of an industry, from natural resources and raw materials to the point of production, as well as distribution, publicity, and retail sales, along with the extension of credit to facilitate these sales, effectively resides in fewer and fewer hands. Beyond this, the system is made concentric through the purchase of various firms that are rationally connected to those aspects of production in which a given corporation is involved—a congealing factor that becomes an additional impetus toward vertical integration. And all of this is accompanied by a voracious propensity for conglomeration as companies in apparently unrelated businesses are horizontally invested in, or bought outright, by those hegemonic corporate institutions that are increasingly what a conservative rationalism is about.

The result is a ramifying system of takeovers, buyouts, and mergers—whether "leveraged" (that is, on margin), "hostile," "friendly," or in whatever guise—an order of interlocking directorates, de facto trusts and holding companies, and consolidated wealth accumulation which eliminates price competition and that moves toward what, early in the twentieth century, some warned would become "the trust of trusts" and Woodrow Wilson assailed as "the combination of the combinations."[9] Corporate names may change along with "reorganization," but this precisely represents a movement toward plutocracy which, to be sure, is occasionally interrupted by the introduction of new industries based on new technologies: a situation wherein a fair number of relevant firms will, for a while, actually confront each other through price competition. Yet the duration of such episodes is short, and notably more so as the centralizing imperatives of modern technology become more entrenched, volatile, and avaricious in their reach.

None of this, of course, bears any resemblance to an order of "perfect competition" wherein prices articulate the simultaneous vagaries of supply and demand and the more-or-less responsive actions of those immersed in a market of many sellers and many buyers—a world of "rational" entrepreneurs and workers arrayed in price struggles with themselves and each other, and in which investment automatically flows to markets wherein supply is low relative to effective demand—that which is at the core of the great material promise of capitalism that justifies the human and environmental devastation by which its alleged presence is so often accompanied. [10]

Contrary to the semantic reassurances of economists about imperfect competition, which insist that a price-competitive market actually exists when the evidence says it does not, the randomness of a free market is the last thing that those who run a postindustrial America desire or, in fact, can tolerate. When much is centralized, much is at stake, and those who manage private bureaucracies with vast public effect seek the assurances of stability. The uncertainties of price competition are plainly too dangerous to bear. People who make corporate decisions think they cannot afford an insufficient predictability, even over the moderately short term, in regard to pricing and, more significantly, to the rate of profit that is invariably written into any price agreement.

Marx is often accused of being naive because he overlooked the mitigating influence of imperialism in proclaiming that a proletarian consciousness would lead to socialist revolutions in advanced industrial countries. But this is conjecture, not theory, and the most cogent contributions of Marx emanate from his theoretical efforts, not his doctrinal projections. Accordingly, he was far from wrong in pointing out that, while the capitalists will never create socialism, it is the capitalists themselves who literally socialize the mode of production. Such is a world wherein liberals become conservatives and if actual capitalists are in short supply the managers will have to do.

* * *

The official fiction is that corporate policies on pricing and profit rates express an obligation to their employees and, in the final analysis, a fiduciary responsibility to the financial interests of the stockholders. However, those who run the industries that now drive the American economy, while they are almost always also stockholders, are to no small degree motivated by the demands and opportunities of their managerial positions. Hidden within a mélange of financial products yielding an opaque configuration of innumerable kinds of derivatives, structural investment vehicles, private and national sovereign wealth funds, foreign currency swaps, junk bonds, and collateral debt obligations, along with their corporate connections and disclaimers, this is not the world of Adam Smith—it is the Byzantine labyrinth of Franz Kafka. [11] Still, the densely bureaucratic maze of relationships and legalities that constitute a corporate conservatism is held together by a deep loyalty to the liberal idea that human beings possess an insatiable appetite to own and control productive property.

This is one possible realization of the Enlightenment. In America, it becomes a surrogate for the democratic dream, although it requires no great intellectual leap to surmise that it imposes an ideological need for power over the labor that creates property, as well as over the labor which is required to then render it productive and salable. That managers are hired—and hire themselves—for this purpose; that they autocratically reign over what have been referred to as "private governments"; [12] are propositions too consistently confirmed by the evidence to be open to much debate. In brief, the logic of the liberal Enlightenment patently eventuates in the arrival of a conservative Enlightenment of corporate supremacy.

That commercial ambition is consistently supported by a variety of governments in the United States is not difficult to understand. Regardless of the antitrust laws, and other progressive attempts to protect the free market, the business of America truly is not capitalism, but business. It always has been, as the provisions of the Constitution, and the policies they inspire and support, abundantly affirm. Within the resulting order public officials do not often have to be bought. After all, they too belong to a culture that proclaims pecuniary ambition to be the catalyst of productivity, individualism, opportunity, success, and progress. Hence the presiding values and attitudes—which are simply unconscious values—that saturate a liberal society insist on a premier allegiance to those substantial rates of profit that presumably reveal contributions to enhanced economic efficiency. It is this which yields, merit and, despite liberalism itself, the hegemonic influence of monumental market power.

Indeed, the concentration of American economics has been abetted and rendered more legitimate by the federal government since the first administration of George Washington in 1789, and state governments have typically not been too reluctant in this regard. The destiny of the United States, was to be a great commercial republic, a goal avidly advanced by Alexander Hamilton when he was Secretary of the Treasury as promotionalism, a quasi-mercantilist policy through which the tendency of accumulated capital to multiply itself would be officially assisted by the general government. This is the same ideological perspective that by 1886 allowed the Supreme Court to declare that business corporations are not merely legal constructions, but are "persons" under the Constitution, with all the rights which "naturally" pertain. [13] Herein are the permutations of a traditional nexus of business and public policy which leads to what Sheldon Wolin refers to as "the mega-state"[14]—an enormous bureaucratic constellation that is currently most blatant when addressing the global concerns of huge corporate enterprise—"American" or not—especially those involving cost-plus contracts and overruns in matters of military procurement as a purported necessity of an associated foreign policy.

While the domination of public policy by big business is nothing new in America, in certain ways the postindustrial era most resembles that of the late-nineteenth century before the Progressive reaction led to the elections of Theodore Roosevelt, who would regulate the trusts, and Woodrow Wilson, who would break them up under the antitrust laws. Nonetheless, in terms of market power, the last quarter of the nineteenth century, and even the 1920s, was simplistic compared to the current situation. A far greater percentage of the labor force, including that part of it employed in agriculture, is now directly or indirectly employed by gigantic corporate structures and their appendages—with all the attendant pulls on worker loyalty which this implies.

Certainly, that since the 1980s business has turned on workers with an enthusiasm worthy of the 1880s is true. Such has been an era of downsizing and of shipping jobs to countries where labor costs are cheaper and other business regulations are lax or even totally absent. This also may ease. Yet, whether or not it does, popular support for the property rights of a privately corporatized system will probably remain strong in America precisely because the option of socialism is culturally perceived to be a foreign idea which poses an unacceptable threat to the liberal commitment to equal opportunity and, it follows, to American exceptionalism and the integrity of the national fabric. This is a position which is held to be eminently reasonable. The great commercial corporations, as Adolf A. Berle, Jr. pointed out many years ago, have become social institutions.[15] They now emerge as the primary expression of the conservative Enlightenment and, accompanied by the rhetoric of inevitability, these institutions become more firmly entrenched, along with their much-admired technological genius and material largesse.

The evidence of polls and elections indicates that this portrayal of reality, as well as its controlling abstractions, infuses the outlook of American majorities, deeply infiltrating the policy content of their will. As always, the values, attitudes, and perceptions that reverberate within a dominant ideology cannot be avoided. Regardless of who actually wields the authority of public office, what emerges is a conservative configuration of corporate liberalism masquerading as a democracy.

* * *

Thus camouflaged by the cloak of the people's capitalism, the triumph of liberal ideology in the United States effectively translates American politics into a worldwide quest for corporate gain. In a less-conscious yet more cogent manner, it reveals a competition for the status, power, and privilege that wealth commands when the private acquisition of money is perceived to harmonize with a contribution to productive efficiency.

Yet these prevailing truths slowly become less compelling to some who adhere to the liberal tradition. Going back to their doctrinal roots, they worry about the dangers to personal liberty which they are convinced are automatically embedded in aggrandized economic power. Nevertheless, the language and the consequent set of conceptions that control a liberal worldview critically impede any serious attempt to deal with what, at some level, may be understood because it fails to confront the actualities of contradiction.

The result is a dual mentality which habitually applauds both market forces and the impressive wealth and productivity of corporate America even while it remains persuaded that the financial leverage of gigantic corporate enterprise will be immediately transformed into the unchecked authority of a single faction—a phenomenon which, within the liberal pantheon, must unleash the natural human disposition toward tyranny. Trapped within one of the central paradoxes of their own consciousness, many liberals become more troubled by the fusion of business interests and the state, which they often wrongly apprehend to be a recent development, a situation wherein citizenship is transformed into the right to be a consumer and to occasionally provide an audience for the few who actually engage in public action. Some even worry that the possibilities of fascism are implicit in a postindustrial order.

Still, they seldom notice that all of this is a logical outcome of their commitment to the liberal version of the Enlightenment as the market society: a certainty about the permanence of human greed; a demand for an unending amplification of productive efficiency; and the associated necessity of the private ownership and control of productive property. In short, they fail to address the doctrinal foundations of an ideology which infuses their definition of reason and that imposes those pervading truths which precisely encourage a culture of liberalism to cede legitimacy to a conservative system of corporate power.

NOTES

1. Cf., Daniel Bell, "The Social Framework of the Information Society," in *The Computer Age: A Twenty-Year View*, ed. by Michael L. Dertouzos and Joel Moses (Cambridge: The M.I.T. Press, 1979), pp. 16–11, and, in particular, 168.

2. Bell, *End of Ideology*, especially, pp. 393–408 and 409–47, and Fukuyama, *End of History*, are instructive. So is Fukuyama, "End of History?," *National Interest*, Summer 1989, pp. 3–18, both cited supra, chap. 1, n. 8 and n. 9.

3. Adam Smith, *An Inquiry into the Nature and Causes of the Wealth of Nations*, ed., with an intro., notes, marginal summary and an enlarged index by Edwin Cannan, with an intro. by Max Lerner, Book 5, "Of the Revenue of the Sovereign or Commonwealth" (New York: The Modern Library, 1937), pp. 653–768, and, in particular, 712.

4. Cf., C. Wright Mills, *White Collar: The American Middle Classes* (New York: Oxford University Press, 1953), in regard to what extent a free market was ever a reality in the United States.

5. John Kenneth Galbraith, *The Affluent Society* (Boston: Houghton Mifflin Co., 1958), p. 156 and passim; John Kenneth Galbraith, *The New Industrial State* (Boston: Houghton Mifflin Co., 1967, chap. 19, "The Revised Sequence," pp. 211–18, and, in particular, p. 212

and passim, capitalized for emphasis in its first usage; and Galbraith, *Affluent Society*, chap. 9, "The Paramount Position of Production," pp. 121–38.

6. A term formulated, or, at least, popularized, by Vance Packard, *The Waste Makers* (New York: David McKay Co., 1960), p. 54 and passim. Also, cf., Vance Packard, *The Hidden Persuaders* (New York: David McKay Co., 1957), "Psychological Obsolescence," p. 21 and passim, and "Planned Product Obsolescence," p. 172.

7. Thorstein Veblen, *The Theory of Business Enterprise*, with a prefatory note by Joseph Dorfman and a review by James Hayden Tufts (Clifton, NJ, 1973), p. 32 and passim.

8. The earliest articulation of this term may be found in John Kenneth Galbraith, *American Capitalism: The Concept of Countervailing Power*, rev. ed., The Riverside Press, Cambridge (Boston: Houghton Mifflin Co., 1956), chap 9, "The Theory of Countervailing Power," pp. 108–34, and, in particular, p. 111 and passim, italicized for emphasis in its first usage.

9. Woodrow Wilson, *The New Freedom: A Call for the Emancipation of the Generous Energies of a People*, with an introduction and notes by William E. Leuchtenburg (Englewood Cliffs, NJ: Prentice-Hall Inc. 1961), p. 112 and passim.

10. Hannah Arendt, *On Revolution* (New York: The Viking Press, A Viking Compass Book, 1963), pp. 219–20.

11. As, for instance, in Franz Kafka, *The Castle*, trans. by Willa and Edwin Muir, with additional materials trans. by Eithne Wilkins and Ernst Kaiser, with an Homage by Thomas Mann, definitive ed. (New York: Alfred A. Knopf, 1959) and Franz Kafka, *The Trial*, trans. by Willa and Edwin Muir, rev., and with additional materials trans. by E. M. Butler, illustrated by George Salter, definitive ed. (New York: Alfred A. Knopf, 1960).

12. The best-known formulation of this is found in Grant McConnell, *Private Power and American Democracy* (New York: Alfred A. Knopf, 1967), p. 5 and passim, and, especially, chap. 5, "Private Government," pp. 119–54, although McConnell makes no claim that the formulation is his own inspiration, ibid., p. 129. For an earlier use of this term, cf., Franklin D. Roosevelt, "Campaign Address at Chicago, Ill: 'It Was This Administration Which Saved the System of Private Profit and Free Enterprise'," October 14, 1936, no. 176, in *The Public Papers and Addresses of Franklin D. Roosevelt*, with a special intro. and explanatory notes by President Roosevelt, ed. by Samuel I. Rosenman, 13 vols. (New York: Random House, 1938), vol. 5, *The People Approve*, pp. 480–89, and, in particular, "a kind of private government," p. 487.

13. *Santa Clara County* v. *Southern Pacific Railroad Co.*, 118 U.S. 394 (1886), especially note the "syllabus," pp. 394–97, and, in particular, pp. 394–95.

14. Sheldon S. Wolin, no. 3, "Elitism and the Rage Against Postmodernity," pp. 47–65, in Sheldon S. Wolin, *The Presence of the Past: Essays on the State and the Constitution*, The John Hopkins Series in Constitutional Thought, ed. by Sotirios Barber and Jeffrey Tulis (Baltimore: The Johns Hopkins University Press, 1989), p. 64 and passim, quoted for emphasis in its first usage.

15. Cf., Adolf A. Berle, Jr., *The 20th Century Capitalist Revolution* (New York: Harcourt, Brace and World, 1954), wherein "the modern corporation," p. 9, is conceived of as "a social institution in the context of a revolutionary century," p. 24, and, more generally, p. 9 and passim, a phenomenon which is central to "the revolutionary capitalism of the mid-twentieth century," p. 9, although how corporate production is transformed into a variation of "capitalism" is not clear. However, also see Adolf A. Berle, Jr., *Power without Property: A New Development in American Political Economy* (New York: Harcourt, Brace and Co., 1959), and, in particular, pp. 19 and 26–27, and Adolf A. Berle, *The American Economic Republic* (New York: Harcourt, Brace and World, 1963), especially p. vii and passim, and, more generally, chap. 1, "The Fragmentation of Economic Concepts: Property in Analysis," pp. 19–35, chap. 4, "'Free Market'—Friend or Menace?," pp. 76–84, chap. 6, "Assumption of Responsibility by the Political State," pp. 95–99, chap. 9, "The Controlled Markets," pp. 137–44, chap. 10, "The Free-Market Sector: Industry and Its Concentration," pp. 145–62, chap. 12, "The Welfare State: The Socialized Sector," pp. 176–85, and "Conclusion," pp. 213–18, wherein some effort is made to distinguish capitalism from a corporate order.

Chapter Three

The Romantic Assault on the Enlightenment

Among those who detect the possibilities of fascism in America, some would maintain that its roots reside in that concentration of business interests which epitomizes the necessary direction of capitalism in its more advanced and corporate stage. This, they often contend, is reflected in a political system that offers nothing more than a choice between a conservative party that opposes any restraints on the pursuit of the bottom line, and a liberal party that pays a bit of homage to the more unfortunate side effects of the bottom line, to which it is, however, equally and fundamentally committed. But the matter is far more complicated than this.

* * *

The Black Shirts. The Brown Shirts. The Green Shirts. Fascism is generally associated with the Italian and German experiences during the second quarter of the twentieth century, with subsidiary attention paid to simultaneous developments in Eastern Europe and France as well as to certain elements of the Falangist episode in Spain. By and large, those who attempt to analyze these movements approach them from the perspectives of psychology and social psychology, often perceiving them as uncommon pathologies which strangely intruded upon otherwise more rational societies. Accordingly, they are considered to manifest the less desirable regions of the human psyche which can spring forth at any time and in any place—a view which frequently emphasizes the fact that the Nazis captured the government of the most educated country of the time, while seldom noting that anything beyond a minimal education in the Germany of that era was the special preserve of the very few. Or they are attributed to the economic conditions in these countries. Or even to the elevation of reason as the increasingly consolidated authority of the modern bureaucratic state, leading to that general political alienation which Max Weber had forecast would be a major consequence of the Enlightenment itself. But they are rarely examined as the realization of ideas that may be far more normal than is usually admitted—as persistent ingredients of the human struggle to make sense of what to many appears as a random and chaotic world within which a sense of powerlessness is rampant and pervasive.

* * *

From the perspective of political philosophy it is standard to assert that fascism and Nazism signify little more than an opportunistic, eclectic, and even illogical mélange of more acceptable formulations. And in many important ways this is true. However, they also contain a coherent intellectual core which is rooted in agreements with, and distortions and rejections of, identifiable theoretical and doctrinal contentions that have long commanded a respectable hearing in the pantheon of Western thought. For instance, the Fascist and Nazi portrayal of the organic oneness of the nation is not exactly a novel idea, receiving its modern voice in the writings of Jean-Jacques Rousseau as well, of course, of Edmund Burke. Thus, for Burke, the nation-state is conceived of as a discrete and fundamental reality that must adhere to its own historical nature—to the seamless web of its own unique traditions— a fabric that must never be violated if the national promise is to be realized and its obligations to the living, the dead, and the yet to be born fulfilled. Here the normative essence of all politics becomes the integrity of the nation itself, a matter which is ultimately discernible only to a talented few who possess an inborn capacity to feel its interior substance.

In fact, the further Burkean assertion that all those variables which comprise the texture of a society are organically and historically entwined may be a useful contribution to any attempt to empirically comprehend the convolutions of the human experience. At the very least, it could offer a sensible alternative to the mechanistic outlook of liberalism, which perceives social, economic, and political systems as separate from one another and, in themselves, as nothing more than the atomistic collection of the human particles of which they are composed: an intellectual posture that allows nothing to be greater than the sum of its parts—wherein there can be no gestalt—and, in the final analysis, no actual system. Still, arguments are habitually employed in ways never intended by those who first profess them, and people are attracted to specific points within an array of doctrinal and theoretical positions in different times and situations. It is in this sense that the Fascists and Nazis extol the Burkean mandate that what constitutes the truth of a nation must be respected—emphasizing the glories of a past that recedes into the very origins of the national history—however fabricated such origins may or may not be.

Furthermore, much as Burke insists on a government of self-selecting elites, so the reactionary champions of fascism and Nazism—who seek not what exists, but the restoration of a more authentic status-quo ante— turn this proposition into rule by the Party and, finally, by a paramount leader. To this extent, these movements are patently conservative. They also imbibe the philosophical Romanticism that informs the European conservative tradition. This necessitates a deep suspicion of rationalism and empiricism along with the insistence that the search for truth must ultimately be rooted in the proper content of emotion and feeling, a search which is reserved strictly for the very few. Yet these movements also reflect a more egalitarian development: an antirational nationalism that begins to infuse Europe in the nineteenth century—and that transforms what Burke had depicted as the organically connected elements of the national tradition into a oneness which emerges as an organism that is literally alive and has a will. Additionally adopting, and distorting, an earlier liberal vocabulary of rights which was intended to apply only to individual human beings, the Fascist and Nazi vision propounds that the state itself possesses those supreme rights within which all other rights are subsumed.

It follows that the state becomes the primary articulation of the nation. This necessitates a right of the government to protect itself, since damage to any part of the organism is deemed to be detrimental to the purity and continuation of the national existence. Through this blatant violation of original intent, the liberal conflation of state and government is transmuted into a nation personified by the state, even while the nation is no longer merely a territorial entity but is now a regime whereby that entity is ruled.

* * *

In their initial stage, those who are convinced that they compose a nation because they presumably share a history, a language and, especially, a culture, whether or not its members actually control a particular territory, set out to attain a state—both as suzerainty over a geographic region and as a government. Then what has become a nation-state may well embark upon a venture to save or civilize humanity—that is, to make the world, or as much of it as possible, into a replication of its own essential being.

Such claims are seldom static. To their proponents, it nearly always becomes axiomatic that a particular nation-state represents higher and more desirable qualities than those found elsewhere, and that this imposes on it a moral obligation to project these qualities into a larger arena—a burden which is integral to the fact of superiority and that infers a mission which it is the destiny of the nation as state to fulfill. Often referred to as nineteenth-century European nationalism, this typically congeals into an ideology that, in its more advanced stage, frequently finds an outlet through colonial, imperial, or military expansion, or by any combination thereof.

Fascism and Nazism are manifestations of nationalism in both of these stages: the demand of a self-proclaimed national people to possess its own land and to govern it through a state, along with the subsequent obligation of this state to spread the good news of its national genius to as much of the globe as can be subsumed into the superior truth and morality of its intrinsic personality. If progress of this kind is to be achieved, all that liberals consider to be private must become public, and the energy of the national people must be fully channeled into consolidation at home while simultaneously assuring that the civilizing function of the state extends beyond the confining restrictions of its present borders. This involves a policy of economic autonomy. It also encourages a population increase that is in no sense a private matter. Exceeding a liberal concern for the additional labor required for greater material production; for the expanded markets to absorb it; and for enhanced levels of profitability, this is ultimately a policy that seeks to provide the planet with more people of a superior type.

Aspects of this aspiration are, of course, not unknown to other instances of the later stage of nationalism. The mission of Japanese racial "purity" "to place the whole world under one roof,"[1] "the white man's burden" of the British Empire, and the "manifest destiny" of the United States—subsequently incorporated into a desire to "save the world for democracy"—are also rooted in "obligations" which predictably flow from an assumption of national superiority. To be sure, these are perspectives that could merely result in an eager willingness to stand as an example for the rest of humanity to emulate. Accordingly, while an economic imperialism supported by armed force is no stranger to American foreign policy, this more placid approach, advanced by, among others, Thomas Jefferson and Abraham Lincoln, nonetheless contends that, at a minimum, that which is better must serve as a model for mankind, suggesting that the claims of the Enlightenment are far from reticent about their global relevance.

But fascism and Nazism patently exceed the usual parameters of a mature nationalism with expansive ambitions. They are extreme reactions to the very universality of the Enlightenment. If there are rights, the only rights which finally matter are those of the organic nation as it is decisively realized in the personality of the state. If there is life, it is the life of the state that is supreme and, if there is will, the will of every citizen must be assimilated into that of the state which, as the necessary vehicle of national purpose, possesses both a life and will of its own. It is this state which has to be unleashed if people are to ever conquer a discredited liberal materialism which continues to saturate the darker pages of contemporary history and yields the corrosive alienation of a dehumanizing era. For the National Socialists it is the appropriate *Geist* which must prevail: the form of the blood will of the *Volk* as a primary force of history that finds its actualization through physical prowess and, in its most elevated articulation, the confirming experience of war—a necessity of the traditional German push to the East in search of living space, and the essential corrective to the rootlessness and cosmopolitan corruptions of reason and science in the forms of capitalism and Marxian socialism. The avoidance of war, for both fascism and Nazism, is the habit of ailing nations. Military exploits are indispensable to the health of the state. They are the most critical statements of its will.

* * *

What all this induces is the centrality of a particular version of corporatism. The historical mission of the thousand-year Reich is, as Hitler puts it, to act as the culture bearer of civilization. To attain this goal it must be appreciated that human beings are truly alive only when they are fully absorbed into the imperatives of the *Kulternation* as these are carried forward by the inspired actions of the state. Herein is the basis of totalitarianism, Fascist and Nazi style: a perception of the psyche which refutes the feeble possibilities of a liberal individualism—as well as of any group or social class, or of any combination of these, that constitutes less than the totality of the nation. It is corporatism which organizes and hence galvanizes the masses—releasing the genius of the nation and translating it into a sublime force of history. It is only this which permits all who are legitimate elements of the state to realize their historical purpose.

Indeed, without such integration into the presiding presence of the state, even a superior people are little more than a horde of brutish creatures whose true intentions must be thwarted, and whose energies can never be otherwise channeled into the authentic realization of their will. It follows that the Party and, far more crucially, the premier leader, are nothing other than the spirit of the national people clamoring for an engulfing egalitarianism wherein everyone is shaped into a corporatist sameness—a spirit which comports with and furthers the mission that history intends. Comparable in many ways to other movements of national aggrandizement, fascism and Nazism represent more than a difference in degree—they are clearly different in kind, a fact that becomes most evident in that specific interpretation of corporatism which is essential to the very nature of their significance.

* * *

It is primarily the Italian Fascists who attribute this portrayal of the corporatist state to Hegel, employing a gross distortion of his argument in a rather successful attempt to associate themselves with his substantial influence on European thought. However, for Hegel, government is only a minor element of the State—that is, the actual state of affairs—which indicates the level of ethical development which momentarily characterizes the progressively rational, and, thereby, ethical consciousness of a population. Indeed, the ultimate State becomes a universal configuration of purely ethical human relationships wherein all traces of the contradictions that reveal the receding remnants of anti-ethic have been screened out by the dialectical processes of history.

This is the arrival of the Absolute Idea, a perfectly rational order of human behavior, of which the state as government is merely a minor reflection. It is a condition within which people are rationally equal and, thereby, morally and politically equal; the endlessly stable culmination of the march of reason in the world; much as the egalitarian proponents of what comes to be termed the vulgar Enlightenment had forecast and proposed. Thus, while accepting the liberal equation of reason with morality, a rational existence for Hegel is not elitist. It is, instead, a condition wherein the capacity of human beings to reason is no longer encumbered by any irrational traits within the personality, including the supposedly permanent intractability of the passions that so centrally controls the liberal rendition of the Enlightenment. What emerges is a world within which freedom does not vary among individuals because freedom depends on the equality of an actual connectedness, and until all are truly free none can be truly free to realize their rational faculties. It is this, in the final analysis, which represents the Enlightenment as the tangible and, generally, empirically verifiable unfolding of reason in history.

Still, much as the Nazis twist the will to power and the Superman of Nietzsche into a justification for the expansionist policies of a super race, so did the Italian Fascists earlier contort the conjectures of Hegel into an apologetic for their own ambitions. In this, they follow many nineteenth-century devotees of authoritarian nationalism who turn the ethical and egalitarian content of the Hegelian State into the liberal identification of state with government; then into the centralized repository of all political authority; and finally into a supreme personality which supersedes all competing considerations of ethics and politics.

* * *

Surpassing this, and in a much more pivotal refutation of Hegel, fascism and National Socialism acclaim an epistemology that categorically rejects the efficacy of reason in the human quest to comprehend the meaning of its own experience. Here is the core of the assault on the Enlightenment, one possible result of the Romantic critique of the Age of Reason that can be traced back, at least, to Rousseau, Burke, and David Hume and their search for an order that would permit people to behave in a more natural and, consequently, authentic manner. In this regard, the Burkean formulation of the nation as an organic and discrete entity which can only be discerned through a proper feeling for the national truth permeates the Fascist and Nazi contentions. It is emotion, not reason, which must prevail. But while, for Rousseau, Burke, and Hume, reason remains of secondary utility, for fascism and National Socialism reason leads only to delusion and a dangerous miscalculation of the national will—even as it interferes with the strategies and tactics of a government which manifests that will.

It is precisely Romanticism of this type, or the elevation of unreason, that distinguishes fascism and Nazism from other authoritarian arguments. Those who inhabit the nation-state have to be made aware that reality is not to be found in a universe outside of man, but is that which ramifies from the national feeling as expressed through the will itself. When Joseph Goebbels famously maintained that if a lie is big enough, and repeated often enough, people will believe it, he was, from the point of view of the Third Reich, not quite accurate. The error was corrected by Alfred Rosenberg, who made it plain that if a lie is big enough, and repeated often enough, it literally becomes the truth. That which is so becomes so because it is felt to be so. The purity of the truth is strictly a matter of the purity of the will—and, conclusively, of the action through which this will is realized.

Of course, this requires that the feelings which inform the will must be pure and, unfortunately, there are alien influences within the boundaries of the nation-state that impede the actualization of its purposes. The integrity of the will must be ensured, and this can occur only when foreign elements that may lurk among the national people are suppressed and, preferably, eliminated. These constitute epistemological pollutants which, especially for the Nazis, cannot be tolerated within the organic oneness of a nation populated by a master race—the Jews, Gypsies, and communists, among others, must be expelled, or, as a final solution, eradicated, from Germany, from Europe and then, presumably, from the planet—a Romantic variation of Social Darwinism that even Herbert Spencer might be reluctant to applaud.

* * *

Since the path to truth is never the application of reason to a universe that precedes the observer, but is that which is brought into being by the will of the superior nation, official policy is obligated to suppress the idea that reality exists whether or not human beings know about it. The view that facts must correspond to evidence which accords with the empirical stipulations whereby such evidence, along with the rational propositions that attempt to explain it, are falsified or verified has to be resisted. In short, not only do fascism and Nazism denigrate rationalism. Far more importantly for the contemporary world, they reject the entire edifice of modern science.

Nevertheless, those who speak for these ideas are quite eager to magnify the value of reason when it comes to the establishment of bureaucracies and, for the Nazis in particular, the use and further development of sophisticated technology, especially the technology of war. For the Germans, the mystical beauty of the mission of blood and soil can only be guaranteed by a quite rational Bismarckian policy of blood and iron. In this, the Italians are not far behind. Accordingly, a Romantic yearning for a previous and more pastoral time of feelings and "culture," as contrasted to the cold, rational, and inhuman calculations of materialism and "civilization," exempts the machine as well as war—and the processes and results of the industrial revolution emerge as spiritual expressions of the metaphysics of will and nation. Such is an outlook which has been correctly referred to as "reactionary modernism," a "mixture of cultural despair and fascination with technological advance."[2]

What this must deny, however, is the methodological perspective that makes these feats of technology feasible—a scientific approach to truth that, by definition, can yield only plausibilities or, at best, probabilities. Even more disturbing to the Fascist and Nazi need for certainty is the penchant of science to perceive the universe as uncertain and unfinished: a condition wherein what appears to be static is merely an event within the phenomena of continual motion.

It follows that scientific inquiry hence becomes nothing more than an extreme example of an abstract rationalism which threatens an absolute truth that need not be sought because it is already possessed. While the organizational demands of technological production and application are compatible with an authoritarian system, scientific activity is not, and any serious attempt to engage in science must, therefore, be defined as an impediment to understanding that can only be achieved through the proper will. Every claim to political authority is embedded in an a priori epistemological position, and fascism and Nazism are crucially based on the anti-Enlightenment epistemology of Romanticism. Truth emerges from the feelings. In the final analysis, the entirety of their worldview radiates from this.

* * *

Thus does a definitive notion of technology as corporatism evolve from an accurate feeling for the national will. This is technology as art and, accordingly, as feeling—or, for the Nazis, as the blood truth of the Aryan race as it builds the New Order into a tribute to the racial genius of the German nation. Such a glorification of the emotions is always accompanied by an attack on the mind as a pollutant that invariably subverts the legitimate effort of the corporatist state to augment the mission of the nation. Any residue of a rational search for cause and effect that flows from the premise that events have consequences—that corruption of modern history which has weakened the will of a superior people—needs to be expunged if the civilizing role of the New Rome or the Fatherland is to be achieved. Indeed, what must be created is a human being who is beholden to those capable of feeling the truth of the will, and who can help to bring about its historical fruition by deferring to the few who are elevated by the national people to rule.

* * *

While various nations and, for the Germans, racial nations, differ in the quality of their truth-producing will, there are, according to the Fascists and the Nazis, also critical differences within nations between a leadership whose unique capacity for determining the essence of this truth is not only preferable, but perfect, and the masses, who must be led by those who are innately qualified to perform this monumentally urgent task—those who can establish a system which dissolves the debilitating angst of the many and makes them aware of the emotional substance of their own will. But, beyond this, even among those Party members who comprise this talented elite, there is always one who is the indispensable personification of the national feeling—the *Duce* in Italy, the *Führer* in Germany—and if the Party, or even the national people, ever fail to agree with the ultimate leader about the content of their own feelings, the leader is inevitably correct.

Only in this manner can the new man be expected to arrive. Only thus can corporatist intention be realized. Here is the cruciality of the *Geist* as it finds flawless articulation through the sublime and unquestionable intuitions of the paramount leader—the one who not only serves the nation, but who personifies it and is its conclusive expression. With the leader the corporatist state and, therein, the mass is propelled from the enervation of despair and catapulted into action and its destined role in human affairs—into the achievement of its elected mission as the carrier of a civilization which is worthy of this new man. Such is the Fascist and Nazi rendition of the Enlightenment idea of popular sovereignty.

The elitism here is blatant. Nevertheless, if the sovereignty of the people and the competitive-party elections of the few by the many are wrongly considered to be democracy—as they commonly are—then it becomes—perhaps disturbingly—apparent that the broad support in Europe for fascism and National Socialism comprised a vital expression of the democratic argument. It is in this context that these movements can be perceived as an egalitarian reaction against the aggressive rationalism of capitalist ambition. Moreover, the pervading cultural themes of a post-Enlightenment West are grounded in the apparent compatibility of the values and attitudes of the scientific enterprise with the economic impulses of a globally oriented liberalism. Hence, of still greater significance, is the assault by unreason and will on the transnational community of the very science which has fueled the impressive yield of modern production.

* * *

This, of course, is quite different from other fundamental critiques of the Enlightenment that also propose that reality is a matter of perception. Certainly, existentialism and, more recently, postmodernism lead to a cultural and, ultimately, a value relativism that has had a patent effect on liberal systems wherein the postmodernist fear of the oppression which derives from privileged claims to the truth resonates with substantial credibility. But the last thing that fascism and Nazism can tolerate is relativism. Their understanding of the truth is absolute; this must be accepted by everyone; so must be their contentions about who finally determines these matters. As such, they constitute a far more essential assault on those claims of reason and empiricism that comprise the core of the Enlightenment itself.

Yet, despite their differences, all these ideas are reactions that emanate from an amplifying tension within a culture that acclaims both the egalitarian implications of scientific methodology as an organized endeavor and an elitist system of property inherent to a liberal order. This reveals a confluence of contradictions that brings the issue of democracy to center stage. Indeed, in an age presumably infused with the dire effects of economic reason and the exhilarating possibilities of technical achievement, this is precisely the assertion of the proponents of fascism and Nazism—the antiliberal corporatist state as the historical fulfillment of the Romantic propensities of the sovereign people and, in its own terms, a dramatic articulation of the action of democracy. As such, it expresses an epistemological position that is simply not compatible with science, reasonable public policy, or even the rational pursuit of wealth by large-scale business interests.

NOTES

1. As quoted in John W. Dower, *War without Mercy: Race and Power in the Pacific War* (New York: Pantheon Books, 1966), p. 274.

2. Jeffrey Herf, *Reactionary Modernism: Technology, Culture, and Politics in Weimar and the Third Reich* (Cambridge, UK: Cambridge University Press, 1986), p. 163.

Chapter Four

Democracy and the Idea of Progress

Emanating from the social-contract perspective of the Enlightenment, the idea of popular sovereignty becomes an abstraction of increasing influence. Political authority is thereby held to reside in all the people equally and it is only the will of this which can establish the state. This is a notion that emerges as the normative foundation of a variety of political doctrines, of which democracy is just one. But popular sovereignty is more than an abstraction. It is also tangibly vital because consent, or its absence, by a sufficient portion of the populace, whether this is active or tacit, is what finally creates, stabilizes, or destroys any system of politics. Thus when Marx speculates that democracy is the essential truth of all regimes[1] he is not referring to an actual democracy. Still, his sloppy use of language notwithstanding, the intent of his comment persists. Every stable order is rooted in consent.

Of course, this alone is not democracy. It is not even a doctrine of politics since it fails to stipulate who should govern, and why, and how. Popular sovereignty is simply a principle about the source of authority which underlies numerous political doctrines. It follows that the sovereign people can will into existence any arrangement of authority it desires—or no arrangement at all, if that is its preference. It may create an order within which majorities rule. Or it may not. The people might not want to literally govern. However, those who do only do so with its consent, and whatever government this may yield is, by definition, a legitimate government. Or, as Hannah Arendt notes, the use of force and coercion, always indicates that the agreement necessary to an effective political order is not present.[2] And here is Marx's point. Any system that is at all stable is popular even though, throughout history, they have rarely been democratic.

Although a notion of government by the demos, or the many who are poor, can be found in classical Greek thought, both among the Ionians, some of whom were inclined toward it, and the Athenians, who overwhelmingly were not, the attempt to develop a coherent argument supporting democracy begins with the seventeenth and only arrives with the eighteenth century. Also rooted in Enlightenment assumptions about natural law, the articulation of democracy as a developed doctrine of politics slightly postdates the enormity of the liberal revolution which undergirds the decline of the dynastic economic systems of Europe. Especially after the disruptions of 1848 the result is a civil war within the Enlightenment, a concurrence of arguments that yield a doctrinal tension between liberalism and democracy—a tension which reflects a cultural dialectic that continues to infuse the politics of much of the Western world. For three centuries the liberal outlook has overwhelmingly prevailed, even while being sympathetic to certain views of a rational conservatism to its right and grudgingly ceding ground to democratic pressures from its left.

* * *

Most fully advanced in America by Thomas Jefferson, the democratic proposal pivotally rejects any justification for a regime of one or the few. Yet, in so doing, it actually denies more than it affirms. No thoughtful democrat perceives the general populace as a paragon of political intelligence, or even of virtue. They merely insist that everyone must be thought of as equal and, consequently, as equally qualified to govern as long as none can offer rationally convincing evidence for an assertion of political superiority.

While, for the democrat, political equality does not have to be justified since it does not allow certain people to rule others, any restraint on the authority of all must infer the existence of people who are more capable of governing than others. But to advocate rule by the one or the few or even the many who are politically superior is a special claim for which any reasonable basis is simply not forthcoming, and those who promulgate the idea that some people are special and are, therefore, qualified to rule ought to, at least, support the claim. Otherwise, the authority to speak for the sovereign people must reside equally in everyone.

Moreover, in reference to the question of who should govern, the democrat traditionally moves beyond reason qua reason and becomes quite empirical. At any given point, some will in all probability be more advanced in the development of their equal capacity to discern the natural laws and, accordingly, what is rational, moral, and true, transforming this capacity into an unequal rational ability. Accordingly, "those talents which nature has sown as liberally among the poor as the rich, but which perish without use if not sought for and cultivated"[3] will lead to differences about what is reasonable. However, without publicly verifiable or falsifiable material evidence of even a momentarily superior qualification, it must be assumed that all are currently the same in political ability and that the influence of each should be identical in the making of decisions that affect more than themselves. In this manner, short of unanimity, and if government is necessary, the observable reality of disagreement results in rule by the greater number as the only scientifically acceptable approach to the question of how political authority ought to be distributed.

Hence the sovereign people ought to govern themselves simply because no one can be considered to be more capable of doing so than anyone else, whatever their alleged talent,[4] or experience, or both. From this flows the democratic idea of self-government, wherein if all who are equal do not agree, the only option is voting; each having reached a presumed age of civic ability being eligible to vote; and each to be afforded an equal weight in the making of public policy, which becomes the concrete expression of the will of the greater number. When a controversy is finally boiled down to two possibilities, the result has to be the wielding of unchecked political authority by one more than half of those voting. This is simply the logic of the matter. What emerges is the principle of majority rule.

* * *

Within such a system, to insist on a priori ethical standards to which a majority must adhere is to contend that these standards are more vital than rule by majorities—a conundrum which can be avoided only when majorities happen to concur with these stipulations. Yet if a majority fails to respect them—and if an ineffective standard is not a standard—then authorized action must be taken either by everyone, or by less than a majority of everyone, eventuating in a probable denial of the principle of political equality as well as a blatant violation of majority rule. That is, in the absence of unanimous agreement, the result has to be minority government, at least in regard to matters which are perceived to be binding by those who presumably best know what they are.

This is a view that often favors majority rule as long as the majority is not ethically wrong, a posture which must infer that one or, more frequently, a few, are best able to discern the public good and, therefore, as the representatives of the will of the sovereign people, qualified to instruct a majority as to if and when it is correct. And it must follow that if they find the errors of the majority to be significant, they have to be authorized to block the effect of majority decisions since this is nothing less than their ethical obligation—an antidemocratic argument that is the basis of all the two-thirds and three-quarter provisions in the United States Constitution.

Plainly, a fear of instability, or what some see as chaos, or anarchy or, perhaps, revolution, persistently animates those who would impose limitations on majorities—although they not infrequently have trouble applying their concerns to the few, or even the one. Moreover, when these standards involve a notion of rights, and since it is quite conceivable that a majority might intrude on the rights of others, many democratic thinkers become enmeshed in the so-called dilemma of majority rule versus minority rights. Still, it is important to note that natural rights are a liberal conception and, while Jefferson used the language of rights, he well understood that, in the final analysis, democracy is not a doctrine of rights, but of power. Thus the presence of rights within a democratic order, and precisely what they are and who possesses them, must be established by the very majority that may deny them to some or even declare that they do not exist at all. For instance, if a right to vote is so established by a majority, only it can determine who has this right, and to what extent. A majority could even dictate that majorities shall no longer govern, and to nullify this through the authority of less than a majority is to once again abrogate the principles of political equality and majority rule—a situation wherein a democracy would cease to exist.

To be sure, the egalitarian premises of democracy can also lead to the doctrine of anarchy—a condition within which every person governs themselves and no one else. Here there can be no public action without unanimity and, if there is unanimity, no public action is required since when all agree the decision is already made and, it should be noted, decisions of majorities can be vetoed by the few or even by one. Given a commitment to popular sovereignty and political equality, this is a logically sustainable position.

However, democrats are not anarchists. Since the empirical actuality is that people seldom agree, they are convinced that government is required and that this must lead to rule by majorities if political equality is not to be violated. Thus, when Edmund Burke disparaged democracy as merely being "told by the head,"[5] he was correct. But then Burke was an unabashed elitist, and some variation of social-class, or elitist, or, more mildly, elite rule are, of course, the traditional alternatives to majorities.

* * *

Yet there is more to democracy than the principles of popular sovereignty and political equality which find their operative application in the arithmetic principle of majority rule. And, as already suggested, the democratic argument does not laud government by majorities as much as it consistently represents a critique of a long history of special claims to govern. Nevertheless, it is also true that the Jeffersonian outlook did comply with the eighteenth-century notion of perfection—a "radical" position generally associated with particular French formulations which some now term the "vulgar Enlightenment,"[6] and which projected an equal rational capacity into the equality of a fully actualized rational ability of everyone: a world of reason wherein the laws of nature would be totally discovered by all and each would act accordingly in a completely egalitarian and harmonious manner.

The core of the democratic formulation, however, is not a concern with the actual attainment of perfection, but the conviction that the better lights of the human species evolve historically. Accordingly, Jefferson comprehended the rational improvement of human beings through the education of civic involvement as a permanent process of increasingly manifest emergence—the revolutionary essence of his argument which continues to afford hope to many and that accounts for the power of its persistent appeal. Indeed, beyond all discussion of principles, logic, and a governing apparatus, what remains significant for the world is the insistence that people, including majorities of people, have not arrived, but are in the process of arriving, and probably always will be. It is this which most crucially distinguishes the democratic position from the dire certainties of liberals and conservatives about the static and inegalitarian consistencies of human nature and additionally, for liberals, the antirationalist passions of even the best of the species.

As distinguished from both liberalism and conservatism, democracy, despite its necessary commitment to majority rule as a system, is finally an argument for human emergence as a process. It follows that the positive possibilities within people are not an achievement to be admired: they constitute a goal to be sought after—and the catalyst of this motion is action in the polis. In short, for the democrat, an "end" to history is unlikely, a proposition, not incidentally, which is patently revealed in Jefferson's insistence "*that the earth belongs in usufruct to the living*': that the dead have neither powers nor rights over it."[7] As mentioned, this is a perspective which dictates that the will of a past majority cannot be allowed to interfere with the ability of a present majority to act in concordance with its enhanced understanding of the laws of nature.

Despite his confidence or, perhaps, his hope that majorities will act in a reasonable manner, these are considerations which centrally inform the Jeffersonian contention that the operative majority must always be the majority of the moment—that a majority of yesterday, or even of their offspring, cannot rule a majority of today, and that a majority of today cannot control a majority of tomorrow—a proposition which becomes articulated as the argument for continuing majorities. In fact, while not usually designated as a principle of democracy, the affirmation of continuing majorities is nothing less than a necessary extrapolation of those principles which infuse the entirety of the democratic perspective. Anything else would usurp the essential postulates of democracy: popular sovereignty, political equality and, most overtly, majority rule as they pertain to any specific situation.

But, far more significantly, it would interfere with the rational development of the species. Herein resides the deeper foundation of Jefferson's adherence to the supremacy of continuing majorities, a view—despite his anarchist tendencies also expounded by Thomas Paine as a logical extension of majority rule itself—which attempts to ensure that the actions of past majorities, or a concern about future majorities, does not restrict the immediacy of self-government.[8] Majorities of the past have had their chance; those of the future presumably will have theirs; and total authority should always be in the hands of the present majority. For the democrat, such a condition is instrumental to progress itself.

This is an assertion which may well disturb those of a liberal or conservative disposition. At the very least, it will probably make their fundamental elitism quite clear. Informing it is the view that phenomena are ultimately not form but process, a conception favored by certain of the Ionian Greeks, as opposed to the pervading Athenian and, eventually, Western commitment to the reality of form, including forms of government, as a permanent condition. Consequently, if for liberals and conservatives the intrusion of continuing majorities can only yield an unsettling instability, for democrats its abiding value is as a vehicle of human emergence. Not surprisingly, it is Jefferson who wanted a revolution and then, more moderately, a constitutional convention, every nineteen years,[9] although it has been popular in times of liberal retrenchment to interpret this component of his thought as a threat to progressive politics.

Still, in apparent conflict with all of this, there is the Jeffersonian advocation of "a natural aristocracy"[10]—conceived of as those who have furthest translated an equal capacity for reason into a temporarily superior rational ability and who, for the moment, are most qualified to guide humanity along the road of the rational progress as formulated by the Enlightenment. This, to be sure, is an undemocratic proposal for leadership. Still, it is one which must dissolve as it encourages the generality of human beings to move closer to a greater- and-more-equal level of rational development. While, for Jefferson, this process can probably never reach perfection, and the nondemocratic state will probably never wither away, it will eventually yield an order wherein all have at least attained an equal ability to govern.

There is no elitism here, no claim of an inherently superior capacity on the part of some to rule others. In the final analysis, however, Jefferson could not really tolerate the establishment of any kind of governing elite, even if this elite was based on the natural quality of reason as opposed to the artificial criterion of wealth; even if it complied with the ancient Greek notion of aristocracy, in which a few rule for the good of all, in contrast to an oligarchy, wherein the few govern only for the good of themselves; and even if it was crucially identified by its commitment to the conclusive dissolution of any need for its own governing position. Thus natural aristocrats were to be elected by majorities which, by definition, were not composed of natural aristocrats—a strange view that is nonetheless mandated by the very logic of a doctrine that persistently refutes the evidential basis for special claims to govern, including those for a natural aristocracy.

It is significant that leadership of this kind and, thereby, the representation of some by others, becomes required only if jurisdictions surpass in size and complexity what is feasible for a democratic order. In brief, it is the magnitude of technological and economic expansion, and the extended juris-dictions and volume of policy decisions that these introduce, which renders democracy impossible. Hence when the prevailing relationships among citi-zens are no longer direct; when the technology that drives economic arrange-ments is not simple and conducive to individual ownership, comprehension, and use, thus placing the information necessary for informed public deci-sions, or even for an intelligent determination of what the issues are, beyond the reach of most people; and when the characteristic conditions of labor move from the autonomy and financial self-sufficiency of small farming to a situation wherein the many are employed by a few and, as a result, are not politically independent, then rule by majorities is no longer a viable proposi-tion. This is because there is a fundamental difference between democracy and a system of mass politics, and the pretensions of liberal-democrats, or even many of those who compose the democratic Left, cannot change this.

All that might remain is the leadership of a natural aristocracy which, for Jefferson is a fall-back position that he also refers to as "a republican, or popular government, of the second grade of purity"[11]—a constitutional sys-tem which, however, in its Madisonian rendition, incorporates representation only partially determined by popular elections. Such a configuration cannot even be thought of as a representative democracy. It is, more precisely, a Lockean system which to some degree involves majorities and, in the in-stance of the United States Constitution, with its predictable stress on rule by competing propertied elites, majorities can hardly be considered to be espe-cially relevant to the actual exercise of political authority. Such is an order that by intention, design, and outcome does not permit an active and egalitar-ian participation in the civic existence by everyone—thus denying an inesca-pable ingredient of the democratic understanding of what it means to be a citizen.

Perhaps it is useful to approach the democratic idea of progress by ad-dressing the historical basis of its understanding of human development. This actually derives from the conviction of certain of the classical Greeks that the good life depends on what they referred to as the telos, a quality which uniquely pertained to every object in the universe; that was thought to literal-ly precede the existence of any discrete entity; and which teleologically affirmed that the a priori purpose of all that exists is the attainment of its own telos. While absolute fulfillment of this purpose was generally presumed to be unreachable, the good life was considered to be that which moved sub-stantially toward its realization. When it came to human beings, the telos, for many influential Athenians, was typically divided into two general catego-ries: the lower type of labor, which was associated with the many, and the higher type of the political, which had relevance strictly to a few.

"Man is by nature a political animal," pronounced Aristotle.[12] However, this included only those qualified by an essential connection to a telos that was in itself political: and it did not mean "is" but really meant "ought" if those who were innately political were to achieve the good life. What was therefore required was total participation in either the greater life of the polis or, for most people, the greater life of labor, if a distortion of the individual and a resulting personal and societal misery were to be avoided. Herein is found the prime meaning of the word totalitarian, a theory of personality which holds that people must totally lose themselves in a life greater than their own if they are to find themselves as integrated beings—to become human, as opposed to being trapped in what is merely an animal-like existence. It is not a description of a state, for which authoritarian is usually the correct designation.

In this manner, the Athenian perspective justifies an arrangement wherein the labor of the many provides the economic wherewithal and—rather conveniently—the leisure necessary for the few who possess the capacity for governing, and who must be exempt from toil so they can expend their energies as they ought to in their appropriate role as citizens. That in ancient Athens most people were slaves, primarily the prisoners of various wars, while the few who were political constituted the governing regime, was really beside the point. Often absurdly referred to as Greek democracy, this was a categorically elitist order. Whatever the disagreements many who inhabited the ruling stratum had with Plato about the viability of the Republic—within which the actualization of the telos of each is literally complete—it was an order critically informed by the Platonic injunction that justice is found, and human fulfillment achieved, only when each is trained to perform their proper function within either polis or labor.

* * *

These are postulations about human nature that, in numerous disguises, lurk deeply within the cultural ambiance of the Western world. And, even though the notion of economic man that lies at the core of the liberal argument fundamentally rejects the notion of the polis as a higher calling, they are ideas that continue to control not only the liberal and conservative portrayals of leadership, but the democratic commitment to majorities as well. Of course, in modern times, they have come to be applied differently. By the eighteenth century, the telos was no longer thought to be present before the fact of being, but was perceived to emerge simultaneously with, and as intrinsic to, each instance of existence. Hence when people are born their telos or, in more current language, their potential, is considered to be born with them, and it is in this sense that the liberal conception of rule by competing economic elites, the conservative depiction of a regime of the trustworthy, and the democratic advocation of an equality of civic power all carry with them the arcane conception of the telos as a pivotal assumption.

However, democrats do not accept the elitism of the Athenian formulation or, for that matter, any other elitist assertion, on the by-now predictable grounds that no special claim to rule has ever been confirmed by evidence, at least not by evidence that is empirically, or even rationally, attained and which, as a consequence, can be publicly shared. Short of this, it must be presumed that the telos of people is universally political; that every human being is equally capable of being a citizen; and that a full engagement in the ongoing history of the polis is equally necessary to the good life for each. Accordingly, everyone is, by nature, a political animal; they are so equally; and the essence of progress is an improvement of the individual personality and, thereby, the species—an improvement which depends on this disposition finding tangible realization through some kind of public involvement and influence.

NOTES

1. Karl Marx, "Critique of Hegel's *Philosophy of Right*," in Part 1,"The Early Writings, 183–844," in *Karl Marx: Selected Writings*, ed. by David McLellan (Oxford: Oxford University Press, 1977), Section 2, "Democracy," pp. 27–30, and, in particular, p. 29.

2. Cf., Hannah Arendt, "On Violence," in Hannah Arendt, *Crises of the Republic* (San Diego: Harcourt, Brace and Jovanovich, Publishers, A Harvest, Harcourt Brace and Jovanovich Book, 1969), pp. 103–98, especially 139–46, and, most particularly, 140–41 and 144–45, n. 67, and Hannah Arendt, *On Revolution*, pp. 149–50.

3. Thomas Jefferson, *Notes on the State of Virginia*, ed. with an intro. and notes by William Peden, Institute of Early American History and Culture at Williamsburg, Virginia (Chapel Hill, NC: The University of North Carolina Press, 1954), p. 148.

4. In regard to rationality, or intelligence, as the "talent" necessary to rule, cf., Bentley Glass, *Science and Ethical Values* (Chapel Hill, NC: The University of North Carolina Press, 1965), pp. 37–46, wherein it is argued that the biological evidence indicates that the probabilities of the inheritance of intelligence is one in seventy trillion, more people than have ever existed. Thus the probabilities are random.

5. Edmund Burke, "Appeal from the New to the Old Whigs," 1791, in *The Works of the Right Honourable Edmund Burke*, ed. by James Prior, Esquire, 7 vols. (London: Bell and Daldy, 1872), vol. 3, p. 92.

6. For the argument that the Federalists were centrally influenced by English ideas and the Antifederalists by French ideas, cf., Vernon Louis Parrington, *Main Currents in American Thought: An Interpretation of American Literature from the Beginnings to 1920*, 3 vol. ed. (New York: Harcourt, Brace and Co., 1930), vol. 1, "The Colonial Mind," pp. 1–413, "Political Thinkers: The English Group," pp. 292–320, and "Political Thinkers: The French Group," pp. 327–56.

7. Thomas Jefferson, "Letter to James Madison," September 6, 1789, in *The Papers of Thomas Jefferson*, ed. by Julian P. Boyd, 20 vols. (Princeton, NJ: Princeton University Press, 1958), vol. 15, p. 392 and passim, quoted in the original, no source provided.

8. Cf., Thomas Jefferson, "Letter to Samuel Kerchival," July 12, 1818, in *Memoir, Correspondence, and Miscellanies from the Papers of Thomas Jefferson*, ed. by Thomas Jefferson Randolph, 4 vols., 2nd ed. (Boston: Grey and Bowes, 1830), vol. 4, in particular, pp. 291–92. Also see Thomas Jefferson, "First Inaugural Address," March 4, 1801, in *The Works of Thomas Jefferson*, collected and ed. by Paul Leicester Ford, Federal Edition, 12 vols. (New York: The Knickerbocker Press, G. P. Putnam's Sons, 1905), vol. 9, pp. 193–200. Furthermore, cf., Thomas Paine, *Rights of Man*, ed. by Claire Grogan, Part 1, (Peterborough, Ontario; Broadview Editions, 2011), p. 73 and passim. This is an essential part of his argument against the claim of

Edmund Burke that the results of the revolution of 1688 comprised a contract in perpetuity to which the English people were bound. Yet while Paine is an egalitarian, he is not an advocate of democracy. This is because of his fundamental contention that the natural rights of each individual can finally be determined only by the individual themselves. Such is a claim that logically leads to anarchy, not to an argument for majority rule. Beyond this, the state of nature as portrayed by Paine is idyllic and leaving it through the invention of private property is depicted as the most fundamental mistake people ever made. This is plainly incompatible with the democratic conception of the historical progress of human beings toward a rational perfection which results from involvement in the political.

9. Jefferson, "Letter to James Madison," September 6, 1789, in Boyd (ed.), *Papers of Thomas Jefferson*, 20 vols, vol. 15, p. 394 and passim, and, in particular, p. 396.

10. Thomas Jefferson, "Letter to John Adams," October 28, 1813, in Ford (ed.), *Works of Thomas Jefferson*, vol. 11, p. 343 and passim.

11. Thomas Jefferson, "Letter to Isaac H. Tiffany," Monticello, August 26, 1816, in *The Writings of Thomas Jefferson: Definitive Edition, Containing His Autobiography, On Virginia, Parliamentary Manual, Official Papers, Messages and Addresses, and Other Writings, Official and Private,* with numerous illustrations and a comprehensive analytical index, ed. by Andrew A. Lipscomb, with Albert Ellery Bergh, 20 vols. (Washington, DC: The Thomas Jefferson Memorial Association of the United States, 1905), vol. 15, p. 65.

12. Aristotle, *Aristotle's Politics*, trans. by Benjamin Jowett, with an intro. by Max Lerner, The Modern Library (New York: Random House, 1943), p. 54.

Chapter Five

The Material Conditions of Democracy

Inherent within the democratic argument is what Jefferson conceived of as the "ward-republic,"[1] a configuration which, importantly, could only be predicated upon certain economic preconditions. This was an order that had to be small in geographic size, sparsely populated, and typified by the stable residence of freehold farmers along with a relatively uncomplicated level of productive technology. Within its jurisdiction human relationships would be overwhelmingly face-to-face and removal from necessary information and specialized expertise in the means of production would not be complicating factors. Central to the Jeffersonian aspiration for America was his vision of a vast array of ward-republics as autonomous, self-governing, agricultural communities extending across a continent wherein people would be attracted to the seemingly endless availability of western land.

Much of this perspective is rooted in Jefferson's conflicted conviction that the material foundation for citizenship no longer requires slave labor. It is the growing seasons, as an evident manifestation of the laws of nature, that supply the leisure for the farmer to truly become a citizen. And it is the financial independence of the small farmer which provides the political independence and the long-term tenure in the same location that are necessary to the real meanings of patriotism and citizenship. The Jeffersonian claim of an entitlement for all adult, white males to 49 acres predicated upon "the fundamental right to labour the earth,"[2] along with the arable land to do so, is one of the most progressive political consequences of the Enlightenment. This far exceeds a liberal assertion of a property right; it is, in fact, a proposal for a system which encourages an equality of the power that emanates from economic self-sufficiency, and which therefore surpasses all other property claims. It is this which crucially infuses the ward-republic and renders it conducive to human progress through the apparatus of self-government by freehold farmers.

That democratic doctrine is historically grounded in an ethical preference for an agricultural world is plain. It is only with Marx that a serious effort to break with this agrarian emphasis develops: an attempt to discover the tangible basis of self-government within an industrializing epoch. This is a perspective that accepts the proposition that the telos of each is equally political and that full immersion in the life of the polis is required if the cultivation of those potentialities that are truly human is to be advanced. In brief, the commune of Marx becomes the industrial—and now, the postindustrial—analog of the ward-republic of Jefferson.

For Marx, however, all are equal in another sense, a sense that introduces a radical conception of labor. People are epitomized by the telos of labor as much as by that of the political. This, of course, is not what Marx delineates as "alienated labor." It is "free labor," or what others have referred to as a calling or vocation, which he identifies as the "objective," genuine, and discrete expression of the inner person.[3] Such is a distinction that is now sometimes articulated as the difference between toil—or even labor itself—and work as that which is essential to being truly human. What it attests to is that the desire for free labor, as well as for civic influence, are both paramount features of human beings trying to shape the contours and substance of a larger world. And these are more than compatible. Free labor and action in the polis are held to be inseparable, suggesting that there is a vast range of ways to act in a political manner, and that to be directly involved in governing is not always the most significant avenue to public effect.

That this is a position that rejects the notion of equality as assimilation into a corporatist conformity is apparent. It also refutes the liberal portrayal of humanity as a mere collection of economic animals subsumed by an endless appetite for pecuniary gain and personal material acquisition. But the economic side of democracy is vital for other reasons. It starkly illuminates the differences between liberals and democrats about elitism and equality and, consequently, about who should rule—arguments that historically emanate from a disagreement about whether people are intrinsically profit- or power-seeking beings and, accordingly, whether they are private or public creatures.

In this, the democratic outlook is more truly classical than that of liberalism, apprehending engagement in the political as an experience that allows movement toward the realization of the telos—a surmise with which conservatives since Plato agree when correctly applied to the appropriate few. Yet only the democrat insists that while everyone is individually distinct they are also commonly human in their search for the nexus of redeeming labor and civic influence as a crucial manifestation of the self. Thus, while democracy argues for equality, it also supports that pluralism of individual variation which is vital to the evolution of the species and is compatible with the need for the power of meaningful labor and public effect which is universally instilled within the otherwise unique telos of each human being.

Such is a view that fits with what an empirically oriented social inquiry has been finding for more than a century: that human behavior invariably discloses a need for power; that power relationships are present as soon as more than one person is involved;[4] that there is no verifiable example of people living in isolation; and that any supposed gulf between the "public" and the "private" is not scientifically supportable. Indeed, the very conception of the private is a social invention that distorts those systemic factors that are critical to the further development and individuation of each personality. As such, the democratic perspective involves a distinction between individualism as an economic phenomenon and individuality as one which involves power and is more essentially human. And it is in this sense that the combination of the notion of free labor as a tangible expression of the creativity of the interior person and the intellectual reflexes that guide a scientific approach to reality render the democratic formulation far more fruitful than those of liberalism or conservatism in promoting any serious investigation into the deeper motivations of the species.

* * *

Within the parlance of contemporary policy disputes in America, this frequently becomes a debate about the proper purposes of the system. Nevertheless, the unstated issue of this debate is whether the endlessly avaricious passions of human beings ensure that material scarcity is forever, or whether there are further and more positive aspects of human nature which are barely tapped because the experience of history has long been mired in a subsuming tale of necessity—a tale that finally can be surmounted once even a moderate affluence becomes a reasonable expectation and people can begin to escape a deeply engrained preoccupation with material survival and wealth accumulation.

Certainly, it is tempting to assert, as the devotees of liberalism and conservatism traditionally do, that the historical willingness of the many to hand over status, power, and political authority to the few or the one is due to a natural and, thus, permanent "immaturity" of "the masses."[5] But within the postulates of the democratic position, this is simply evidence that most people have some distance to go before they can deal with the demands of self-government. Accordingly, the democratic outlook perceives all as citizens in the classical sense of active participation in the affairs of the commonwealth, not as subjects to be ruled by others—no matter how large their pile of material acquisition may be. It further expresses a conviction that a greater equality of public effect can only evolve from an environment within which people are less concerned with the "right" to appropriate property than they are engaged in appropriating their own diverse talents as part of finally beginning to fulfill the demands of their more profound needs.[6]

Hence, even though it is predicated upon the assumption of economic sufficiency, democracy is never an argument for an endless increase in material production—or even consumption—while the ideas of polis and free labor, which are at the core of the democratic position, speak to human needs that are hardly yet realized, but that will presumably become more overt when a certain degree of financial security can begin to be systemically assumed. Inferred is an egalitarian tendency which is always proportionate to a dissolution of economic scarcity—and, importantly, of residual concerns about scarcity—matters liberals are certain can never be resolved and which their policies often attempt to reaffirm. Consequently, in contrast to the democratic advocation of public action, the liberal urges public avoidance and an endless preoccupation with wealth accumulation—an arcane condition that, for the democrat, can persist only for as long as people's idea of who they are knows no other economic and cultural foundation.

And, in fact, as implied by the now well-supported theory of diminishing marginal utility initially enunciated by John Maynard Keynes, even a relative removal from a concern about money will frequently encourage human beings to pursue their deeper ambitions: to seek free labor and civic effect in myriad ways that, in the end, invariably find actualization as power in the polis. What this cogently looks to is the release of those energies which compose what Marx conceptualizes as "species being,"[7] or what Erich Fromm visualizes as people "grasping the world productively."[8] It articulates the long association between the democratic idea of human advance with an understanding of freedom as a slowly emerging phenomenon which is synonymous with an expansion of civic power among increasing numbers of people—as differentiated from, and often opposed to, the liberal stress on those rights which establish an arena into which the authority of government may not intrude.

Often referred to as the distinction between positive liberty and positive freedom and negative liberty and negative freedom, a formulation wherein liberty—or what are really rights—and freedom are actually identical, the easier and more useful categorization is between liberty and freedom[9]—a distinction which illustrates the salient differences between liberalism and democracy. This is because freedom must translate into power not, to adopt the terminology of Fromm, as "power over," but as "power to."[10] Freedom, in this sense, corresponds to the democratic conviction that what constitutes progress is the steady realization of the self through the action of labor within the material context of public engagement[11]—a context which ensures that those who are "led" are those who "lead."

This comprises the real basis of socialism although, in this respect, the democratic focus is never on a greater equality of condition, or result, unless that is what a majority commands. It is, instead, always a focus on an equality of power and authority as this is instrumental to the further and, as yet, little realized possibilities of human beings—a projection that must be distinguished from the unchanging quality of a utopia that can be literally attained. As such, it is a view which resists the cyclical and gloomy liberal version of history, wherein the only acceptable idea of progress is an augmentation of the gross domestic product. For the same reason it also opposes the futility about the nature of most people that centrally informs the equally static and authoritarian absolutes of conservative ideology.

Within contemporary American politics, where a liberal commitment to equal rights encourages the postmodernist claim that facts are nothing more than personal opinions, it would appear that anyone can be a democrat merely by announcing their commitment to the idea of consent. Still, the support of the American people for a liberal government predicated upon the interests of contending entrepreneurial elites, or conceivably, for a conservative regime of a self-selecting superior few, is no more democratic than would be consent to an order rooted in the Romantic intuitions of a self-selecting Fascist or Nazi leadership. Each finally relies on the conception of popular sovereignty to oppose rule by majorities, grounding their assertion of legitimacy in the proposition that those who govern are authorized to do so because of the consent of the governed. Accordingly, while a system wherein the people reign but do not rule[12] complies with popular sovereignty, the real question for the democrat is the content of the prevailing agreements among those who are consenting.

Yet, regardless of every obstacle of habit and certainty, increasing numbers of people, grudgingly or not, follow the impulse to delve further into the unknowns of the universe and themselves—a process through which human beings somewhat less consumed by financial concerns gradually reach for more profound insights into their need for publicly effective power. Accordingly, they become more open to the deeper dimensions and complexities of their own personalities. While, in all probability, this is a process without end, it is conclusively what the radical version of the Enlightenment is about. More to the immediate point, in the face of an overwhelming liberal meritocracy, it expresses that conception of progress which a democratic culture demands.

NOTES

1. Thomas Jefferson, "Letter to Joseph C. Cabell," February 2, 1816, in *The Papers of Thomas Jefferson: Retirement Series*, ed. by J. Jefferson Looney, 11 vols. (Princeton, NJ: Princeton University Press, 2012), vol. 9, p. 437. Also cf., "Ward-republics," in Jefferson "Letter to 'Henry Tompkinson' (Samuel Kerchival)," July 12, 1816, ibid, vol. 10, p. 225, capitalized in the second usage. As a corollary to this, for the argument known as "the Turner thesis," that democracy is only possible in frontier conditions, cf., Frederick Jackson Turner,

"The Significance of the Frontier in American History," in *Annual Report of the American Historical Association for the Year 1893* (Washington, DC: Government Printing Office, 1894), pp. 19–27.

2. Thomas Jefferson, "Letter to James Madison," October 28, 1785, in *The Papers of Thomas Jefferson,* ed. by Julian P. Boyd, 20 vols. (Princeton, NJ: Princeton University Press, 1953), vol. 8, p. 682.

3. Among many other possibilities, cf., Karl Marx, No. 10, "On James Mill," in McLellan (ed.), *Karl Marx: Selected Writings,* pp. 114–23, and, in particular, 121–22.

4. In the sense that *"power* is participation in the making of decisions," Harold D. Lasswell and Abraham Kaplan, *Power and Society: A Framework for Political Inquiry,* Yale Law School Studies, vol. 2 (New Haven: Yale University Press, 1950), p. 75, italicized for emphasis in the first usage. Of course, in reference to the possibility of creatures that act but do not make "decisions," this could be expanded into power as the ability to influence behavior, one's own or anyone else's, regardless of what anyone may think.

5. For instance, cf., Alexander Hamilton, in Hamilton, Jay, and Madison, *Federalist* no. 78, pp. 502–11, wherein apparently "the ordinary depravity of human nature," p. 511, clearly does not apply those qualified for the judiciary and, presumably, for certain other positions of authority as well.On this point conservatives, such as Hamilton, and liberals fundamentally agree. Among the many possibilities, cf., Gustave Le Bon, *The Crowd: A Study of the Popular Mind,* with a new intro. by Robert K. Merton (New York: The Viking Press, Viking Compass Edition, 1960); José Ortega y Gasset, *The Revolt of the Masses,* authorized translation from the Spanish (New York: W. W. Norton and Co., 1932); and Walter Lippmann, *Essays in the Public Philosophy* (Boston: Little, Brown and Co., An Atlantic Monthly Press Book, 1955).

6. For example, Karl Marx, *The German Ideology,* Part 1, trans. and ed. by S. Byazanskaya in Part 1, "The Early Marx," pp. 1–200, in *The Marx-Engels Reader,* ed. by Robert C. Tucker, 2nd ed. (New York: W. W. Norton and Co., 1978), pp. 146–200.

7. Karl Marx, "Critique of the Hegelian Dialectic and Philosophy as a Whole," pp. 106–25, in "Economic and Philosophic Manuscripts of 1844," trans. and notes by Martin Milligan, pp. 66–125, ibid., p. 112 and passim.

8. Erich Fromm, *Marx's Concept of Man,* with a trans. of Karl Marx, *Economic and Philosophical Manuscripts,* by T.B. Bottomore, Milestones of Thought (New York: Continuum, A Frederick Ungar Book, 1992), wherein this is expressed as a matter of man "grasping the world productively, and thus making it his own," p. 29 and passim. For a more developed idea of what is intended here, see ibid., Part 4, "The Nature of Man," pp. 24–43, and, especially, section 2, "Man's Self-Activity," pp. 26–43. Accordingly, "man is alive only inasmuch as he is productive, inasmuch as he grasps the world outside of himself in the act of expressing his own specific human powers, and of grasping the world with these powers," ibid., p. 29, while human progress is that which moves people toward becoming "productively related to the whole world," p. 82.

9. The generally accepted, if somewhat-murky, formulation of this is found in Isaiah Berlin, "Two Concepts of Liberty," in Isaiah Berlin, *Four Essays on Liberty* (London: Oxford University Press, 1969), pp. 118–72, and, especially, pp. 121–22. Much better is the distinction between "liberty" and "freedom" in Arendt, *On Revolution,* pp. 21–8, 129–30, 135, 220–21, 258–59, and 236–37, and, more generally, chap. 3, "The Pursuit of Happiness," pp. 111–37 and passim. Also, cf., Karl Marx and Frederick Engels, *The Holy Family, Or Critique of Critical Criticism: Against Bruno Bauer and Company* (1845), trans. by Richard Dixon and Clemens Dutt, in *Karl Marx, Frederick Engels: Collected Works,* 47 vols. (New York: International Publishers, 1975), vol. 4, "Marx and Engels: 1844–45," trans. by Jack Cohen, Richard Dixon, Clemens Dutt, Barbara Ruhemann, Christopher Upward, and Florence Kelly-Wischnewetzky, p. 131 and passim.

10. Cf., Erich Fromm, *The Anatomy of Human Destructiveness* (New York: Holt, Rinehart and Winston, 1973), pp. 235–67 and passim, and Erich Fromm, *Man for Himself: An Inquiry into the Psychology of Ethics* (New York: Henry Holt and Co., An Owl Book, 1990), p. 88 and passim.

11. In regard to the foundation of the materialist theory of history and its connection to democracy as expounded by Marx, cf., Karl Marx, "Difference Between the Democritean and

Epicurean Philosophy of Nature: With an Appendix," doctoral dissertation (1840–1841), trans. by Dirk J. Struik and Sally R. Struik, in *Marx, Engels: Collected Works*, 47 vols., vol. 1, "Karl Marx: 1835–43," trans. by Richard Dixon, Clemens Dutt, Jack Lindsay, Alick West, Alex Miller, Dirk J. Struik, and Sally R. Struik, pp. 25–107.

12. For a variation of this, cf., Sheldon S. Wolin, *Tocqueville Between Two Worlds: The Making of a Political and Theoretical Life* (Princeton, NJ: Princeton University Press, 2001), pp. 74–75.

Chapter Six

The Problem of Majorities

It is on the basis of the radical Enlightenment and its idea of human progress that the propriety of majority rule becomes significant. Thus in the West, as C. B. Macpherson puts it, and in essential conflict with the market elitism which emerges from the mainstream of the Age of Reason, an emphasis on majorities steadily ramifies as an overlay on what remain, at bottom, the authority delegations of liberal systems. This, he argues, was and is a combination supported by many liberals in an attempt to maintain the established social-class configurations of capitalism—and their positions of power and privilege within them—by constricting the results of "reform" and heading off any inclinations toward socialism.[1]

But there are forces in the world which thwart ambition. If democracy is a manifestation of the more egalitarian elements within the Enlightenment, the central dictate of the Enlightenment itself is that reason and empirical evidence shall take humanity where they will. These insistently amplify into what Ferdinand Tönnies describes as the tension between "*Gemeinschaft und Gesellschatft*"[2]; or what the German intelligentsia portrayed as the struggle between civilization and culture; a tension between a more secular, universal, and cosmopolitan consciousness and one which is parochial, insulated, and mired in the fixed certainties of tradition. What results is a democratic ambiguity which applauds the expansionist tendencies of reason as expressed through the concentration of venture capital, technological innovation, and modern science while nostalgically seeking the presumably self-governing qualities of a presiding localism.

All of this is propelled by a persistent human need for public effect—a need that actually exceeds any form of the state, although democrats traditionally translate it into a state ruled by majorities. Yet this is a proposition that becomes increasingly problematic with the development of modernity.

For instance, as Alexander Hamilton famously notes, the requirement of frequently responding quickly to the behavior of other governments in the domain of foreign policy mandates a consolidation of authority which permits public officials to act with speed, secrecy, and in a unified manner[3]—or what is now customarily referred to as "unity of command." Speed and secrecy are blatantly antithetical to democracy which, even in its representative distortion, has to atomize authority into districts. This institutes government by legislatures—an arrangement which is notoriously slow and usually the last thing from secretive. The stipulation of unity is actually antidemocratic as well since majorities are typically rife with a diversity of perceptions that magnifies as the relevant population expands, even while there is often more than one majority involved depending on how jurisdictions are established. Still, precisely such unity is inherent to the governing of large societies due to the sheer volume, scope, and rapidity that attend the public decisions which these societies engender.

Such are conditions that eradicate any semblance of the Jeffersonian formulation of government by politically independent citizens. Exemplified by the centralizing imperatives of advanced technology, they assure that most people cannot be financially and, hence, politically, independent. Even as entrepreneurs they owe their material wherewithal to an array of corporatized entities which are extensions of, or beholden to, the solidification of capital. This is a situation made more extreme by a corollary movement toward a transnational economic order and the complexities of its global interactions—an expression of the impulse to enhance efficiency by concentrating market power through the often-competing goals of augmented profit rates and organizational growth. In short, as Jefferson's insistence on a multitude of agrarian and autonomous ward-republics makes evident, huge populations and economic constellations of vast productive, distributive, and financial size erase any serious chance for majorities to apply their reason to that necessary information to which the democratic position insists they must have full and equal access. Given these realities, it is likely that majorities—however rational those who compose them may or may not be—will have little opportunity to comprehend the substance of the forces that besiege their existence.

* * *

For fascism and Nazism, the will of the sovereign people is personified by the ultimate leader who is the perfect expression of the genius or racial genius of the nation. And if this application of popular sovereignty is one possible articulation of the conservative outlook, it is also a conceivable result of majority rule. Indeed, those who wield influence in a democratic America precisely attempt to manufacture mass agreements to acceptable truths through the very media which are spawned by the same economic forces that render self-government impossible. The people is then said to consent to these constructions and, thereby, to the continuation of the system which is held to be dependent upon the permanence of this consent.

Under these circumstances, to the degree that the proponents of the radical Enlightenment ignore its deeper and more classical roots, democracy is a doctrine that possesses very little connection to the actualities of power in a postindustrial era. To be sure, there has been a continual extension of the franchise to greater numbers of people; there clearly have been occasions when its exercise led to more egalitarian policy outcomes; and, perhaps exceeding this, the threat of the vote, as distinct from the vote itself has, at times, mitigated actions that serve only the perceived interests of big capital. However, voters must now contend not with a free market, but with a bureaucratized configuration of elite and social-class influence that is inordinately opaque—so much so that those who are supposedly in charge may not themselves fully grasp what they are actually in charge of even as they reflexively cheer on the many in support of democracy. The public consequences of all this are a pervasive removal of most human beings from the relevant facts while democracy devolves into a quasi-popular spectator sport about which increased attention usually is paid during election-season spurts.

Presumably, when the number of sides to an issue is effectively minimized, a majority is empirically observable; heads can be counted and a definitive result announced. If, on the other hand, what is referred to by some as "radical democracy"[4] flourishes only at those moments when the people as a whole seizes societal power, then democracy is merely popular sovereignty and no longer has any association with majority rule. It instead becomes an instance of popular government which, to say the least, is rare: a condition of unanimity which results from a habit of mind that nullifies disagreement, and which would probably ensure that the tyrannies of the one or the few will become more endemic than even Plato thought they would be.

Fearing exactly this, and substituting the conformity of mobocracy for the range of perceptions that actually infuses majorities, liberal democrats look to competitive party elections as a surrogate for self-government. This is as near to a majoritarian position that they are able—or willing—to get. They consequently reject the essential democratic proposition that some can never be represented by others and that the only one a person can really represent is themself. And all the while there is the risk that if people are told often enough that they really govern they might come to believe it, and to find themselves a bit irritated when they discover they do not—a possibility that liberals who would be democrats must assiduously avoid.

Of course, a majority out of touch with reality within a world driven by advanced technology sounds like a recipe for fascism—and there is little doubt that the chips of history largely fall according to the propensities of populations which cannot or refuse to apprehend them. Yet democracy is not rule by plebiscites, or what Theodore Lowi depicts as "an ersatz Bonapart-ism,"[5] and there is no similarity between masses or "crowds" or even "the public," and relatively informed "publics."[6] What Jefferson would think about this is sufficiently transparent because he always accepted the classical distinction between a majority and a mob, which was categorized as a major-ity oblivious to the controlling events of its own time and, for this reason, absolutely not qualified to govern. And, while Jefferson was reasonably sure that the inherent localism and leisurely pace of the ward-republic—or even of a slightly broader localism—would prevent a mob from emerging, he also suspected that the probabilities of exactly this vastly multiplied with the centralizing tendencies of commercial development as reflected in the ratifi-cation of the Constitution.

To apply these arguments to the contemporary world demands a recogni-tion that there is a pivotal difference between an expansionist nationalism as an abstract moral obligation and patriotism as a tactile love of country.[7] Liberalism is an expansionist movement. Under the alias of democracy it would make the world the same in the name of capital, a phenomenon which manifests the civilizing will of the nation itself. But an actual democracy is rooted in patriotism. It is certainly not entranced by the lures of global ambi-tion. In fact, it is likely to be quite parochial because it is grounded in face-to-face relationships and the individuality and fraternity that emanate from hu-man proximity and a tangible sense of place.[8]

The democratic idea of community is predicated upon an egalitarian dif-fusion of civic power and, if this does not typify every community, it may well characterize a vast percentage of small, independent jurisdictions. How-ever, this is a goal which is patently subverted, not only by capitalism, but far more so by the amalgamating imperatives of technological advance. Still, to return to a communitarian analog of the ward-republic, or even to the com-peting entrepreneurial elites of a functioning capitalism, would be to undo the impressive material output that flows from the economic planning that concentration allows. As a result, for democrats to prefer the narrow and conformist attitudes of gemeinschaft and to reject the cosmopolitan outlook of gesselschaft; to attempt to recover an earlier industrial capitalism by advo-cating a retreat from finance capitalism; is, paradoxically, to oppose an es-cape from material necessity—and, accordingly, from the fulfillment of that positive human potential which is the ultimate intention of the democratic argument.

* * *

These are tensions which raise disturbing questions about the cogency of majorities in the modern world. But they are also questions which are gener-ally ignored by most who support democracy, who rightly fix on the formal-ities of voting and on who should be entitled to vote in particular elections, along with the details of their mechanisms and procedures, while wrongly avoiding the issue of rule by ignorance. Nonetheless, electoral activity of this kind has egalitarian value. Even though the problems of information and civic knowledge are pervasive; and that majorities voting to be represented by a few is not democracy; and whether or not people exercise the franchise in a manner that many democrats consider to be rational usually in a liberal America, meaning for their own immediate financial interests—the very act of voting encourages an ethos that moves the culture in the direction of political equality. It thus induces a complicating pressure on the propertied elitism of the prevailing order. Within "the information society"[9] information about the actualities of politics is exceedingly scarce for most people. Yet, because of the myth of democracy, policy must sometimes be explained or, at least, made palatable to the populace and, in this manner, an expanded franchise whittles away at "the ideological veil with which society conceals the true nature of political relations"[10] wherein the substance of power invariably hides.

* * *

All of this speaks to the deeper dilemmas that have always accompanied the radical Enlightenment. To merely insist that a majority ought to rule is blatantly insufficient as a political doctrine. Some claim must be made for its inherent merit. Indeed, a concern about the authoritarian, uninformed, and anti-intellectual tendencies of majorities that will crush the civilizing contributions of the creative minority or, perhaps, minorities, comprises a pervasive theme of Western political contention. It is a theme that any thoughtful proponent of democracy cannot simply dismiss.

There is, for example, the possibility that a ruling majority, national or otherwise, can be perceived—or, more to the point, can perceive itself—as superior, not only to an immediate minority, but also to other majorities that happen to exist elsewhere. That is, any majority can decide that it possesses an elitist or, at a minimum, an elite quality of political wisdom. Indeed, the tradition of American exceptionalism stipulates exactly this. What emanates is a self-anointed role as a model for the rest of humanity and, when this prevails in conjunction with the expansionist economic and military policies of liberalism, it becomes a colonial and imperialist impulse that finds no shortage of self-righteous company in the story of the species. Here is a supposed genius that does not reside in the one or the few: it is found instead in the much-celebrated qualities[11] of American majorities—a celebration that actually resonates less with the Enlightenment than with the Puritan rhythms of a particular brand of elitism, a logical conundrum which historically typifies the major policies of the United States both at home and abroad.

Hence, for more than three centuries, majorities agreed that second-class citizenship for women as well as the peculiar institution of slavery were rational; their perceptions of Native Americans led them to approve of manifest destiny and the policies of extermination and relocation which attended these perceptions; and they more recently supported the unconstitutional internment of Japanese Americans during World War II. They have traditionally been willing to fight wars for democracy that had nothing to do with democracy. In fact, regardless of repeated assurances about the common sense of the American people, it is not irrational to suspect that a majority of them might favor feeling over reason, to say nothing about empirical evidence. These are tendencies, particularly when joined with an aggrandizing global purpose, which can coalesce into behavior that more than a few democrats might be inclined to describe as undemocratic.

Beyond this, when such a combination infuses the worldview of an advanced technical people, the voices of an authoritarian nationalism and its associated corporatism become louder and echoes of the culture bearing and civilizing missions of Italian and German majorities during the Fascist and Nazi years become more distinct. And, while what amounts to a generic American fascism has been most consistently realized—at least so far—when the country is going through one of the periodic Red scares that punctuate its experience, spasmodic episodes replete with proclamations of a national superiority, it is this which may have inspired the query of H. L. Mencken about "how can any man be a democrat who is sincerely a democrat."[12] In brief, there is nothing within the principle of majority rule which guarantees that majorities will adhere to the admonition of the Declaration of Independence to always demonstrate "a decent respect to the opinions of mankind."

* * *

The traditional opposition to democracy is rooted in the conviction that majorities are reflexively moody and monolithic; that they largely act not on the basis of reason and evidence but on that of conformity and habit; and that rule by the many can only result in a suffocating tyranny by the lowest common denominator. If this troubles some who favor "democracy," such is a view that informs most of the respected traditions of political philosophy—including the mainstream of the Enlightenment—more than a few of which, especially in the modern age, are eager to assure everyone that they too are "democratic" even while they are opposed to the "tyranny of the majority."[13]

More realistically, however, what the arrival of the many onto the stage of history really introduces is not majority rule but the negative influence of majorities as a check on elitist claims. Accordingly, if contemporary productive imperatives suppress the ability of majorities to literally govern, popular elections remain necessary to any progressive development. But this is less a matter of illusions about self-government and more about elections being instrumental to a countervailing power which may create crevices in what would otherwise be an impenetrable corporatized fortress. Majorities may often be buying a pig in a poke. Yet, in respect to power and equality, the only thing worse than the many voting is when they cannot vote at all.

Additionally, as Frederick Engels contends, an adequate series of quantitative changes can eventually bring about a qualitative change—a process presently referred to as "punctuated equilibria"[14]—and which might suggest that an institutionalized pluralism, that is long embedded within the liberal commitment to natural rights and government by competing entrepreneurs, might finally escape the elitist core of its own tradition. And, indeed, as the notion of rights becomes broader and more inclusive, the conception of property moves toward a redefinition which increasingly applies to a nonmonetary version of a property in talents, abilities, and aspirations. This encourages inclinations that are more cooperative and even more human in a deeper sense—inclinations that the early proponents of a liberal capitalism clearly did not intend, although some certainly did fear them, as do many of their current devotees.

* * *

In this manner the argument for majority rule promotes those transitions of culture, language, and ideology that always germinate rather glacially. However, its proponents must recognize that, however slow its development, a more egalitarian view of the human potential is usually greeted as an abrupt and unwelcome disruption of deeply respected truths. The power of habit is enormous. Not surprisingly, any serious attempts to implement a greater equality of political authority are predictably met with substantial resistance. Within the struggles which ensue, what is novel is generally distorted and denigrated as a violation of tradition while, if the majoritarian idea becomes at all acceptable, it is often co-opted in support of the status quo.

Thus, whether stated or implied, the reaction of a liberal order centrally betrays a fear that democracy will result in a governing morass of ignorance, mediocrity, and sameness that allegedly characterizes anything resembling populism. But, short of a perfected and universal comprehension of natural law, which the classical democrat projects and then ignores, equality does not have to mean sameness, and differences do not have to mean inequality in regard to the civic value of the myriad and varying talents of human beings.

In the final analysis, the idea of majority rule is analogous to the values associated with procedural due process of law—the purpose of which is not the procedures as much as their utility in the search for the substance of justice in specific cases. Correspondingly, a majoritarian order may enhance what Erich Fromm portrays as the life-furthering as opposed to the life-thwarting inclinations within human beings,[15] an arrangement of civic power which is centrally informed by the dictum that until all are free none are free.[16] That is, although the democratic pursuit of majority rule is not—and never was—a goal in itself, it is necessary, if not sufficient, to the equal and fuller development of the positive powers of humanity. Such claims about the civilizing effects of immersion in the polis, or engagement in the political, are not uncommon in the history of Western thought. But they have been typically applied to the one or the few, and certainly not to the many or to all, and they plainly have not been popular in the United States.[17]

Nevertheless, it is within this context that American democracy emerges as an ideological reflection of the radical Enlightenment, a force that intrinsically resists the economic reason of the liberal Enlightenment and its capitalist and, finally, corporate inferences.

NOTES

1. C. B. Macpherson, *The Life and Times of Liberal Democracy* (Don Mills, Ontario: Oxford University Press, 2112), p. 51.

2. Ferdinand Tönnies, *Community and Society (Gemeinschaft und Gesellschaft)*, trans. and ed. by Charles P. Loomis (New York: Harper and Row, Publishers, Harper Torchbooks, 1963), p. 33 and passim.

3. Alexander Hamilton, in Hamilton, Jay, and Madison, *Federalist*, no. 70, p. 445 and passim.

4. For instance, C. Douglas Lummis, *Radical Democracy* (Ithaca, NY: Cornell University Press, 1996).

5. As remembered from Theodore J. Lowi, Untitled Speech, at the Annual Meeting of the Northern California Political Science Association, San Francisco, California, May 13, 1978.

6. Such as contended, for instance, in John Dewey, *The Public and Its Problems*, 3rd ed. (Denver: Alan Swallow, 1927); Walter Lippmann, *Public Opinion* (New York: The Macmillan Co., 1965); and C. Wright Mills, *The Power Elite* (New York: Oxford University Press, 1956).

7. As suggested in Garry Wills, *Nixon Agonistes: The Crisis of the Self-Made Man* (Boston: Houghton Mifflin Co., 1970), p. 494 and passim.

8. Cf., Wilson Carey McWilliams, "The Machiavellian as Moralist," review of *Walter Lippmann and the American Century*, by Ronald Steel, in *Democracy: A Journal of Political Renewal and Radical Change*, January 1981, p. 103.

9. For instance, cf., Bell, "Social Framework of the Information Society," in *Computer Age*, Dertouzos and Moses (eds.), pp. 16–11, and, in particular, p. 168, cited supra, chap. 2, n. 1.

10. Hans J. Morgethau, "Power as a Political Concept," in *Approaches to the Study of Politics: Twenty-Two Contemporary Essays Exploring the Nature of Politics and Methods By Which It Can Be Studied*, ed. by Roland Young (Evanston, IL: Northwestern University Press, 1958), pp. 66–77, specifically, p. 73.

11. Cf., "those who have abandoned criticism for the new American celebration," C. Wright Mills, *The Power Elite* (New York: Oxford University Press, 1956), p. 25.

12. H. L. Mencken, *Notes on Democracy* (New York: Octagon Books, 1977), p. 212.

13. Alexis de Tocqueville, *Democracy in America*, the Henry Reeve text, rev. by Francis Bowen, corrected and ed. with an intro., editorial notes, and bibliographies by Phillips Bradley, 2 vols. (New York: Alfred A. Knopf, 1976) vol. 1, p. 258 and passim, capitalized as a heading in its first usage.

14. On this, cf., Niles Eldredge and Stephen Jay Gould, "Speciation: Punctuated Equilibria: An Alternative to Phyletic Gradualism," in Part III, "Populations and Evolution," pp. 61–145, in *Models in Paleobiology*, ed. by J. M. Schopf (San Francisco: Freeman, Cooper and Co., 1972), pp. 82–115; Stephen J. Gould and Niles Eldredge, "Punctuated Equilibria: The Tempo

and Mode of Evolution Reconsidered," *Paleobiology*, Spring 1977, pp. 115–51; and Stephen Jay Gould, "Life in a Punctuation," *Natural History*, October 1992, pp. 10–21.

15. Fromm, *Man for Himself.*

16. G. W. F. Hegel, *The Phenomenology of Mind*, trans. with an intro. and notes by J. B. Baille, 2nd ed., rev. and corrected throughout, Muirhead Library of Philosophy (London: George Allen and Unwin, 1949), chap. 4, "The Truth Which Conscious Certainty of Self Realizes," pp. 217–67, and, especially, Part A, "Independence and Dependence of Self-Consciousness: Lordship and Bondage," pp. 228–40. Also, cf., Karl Marx and Frederick Engels, *Manifesto of the Communist Party*, authorized English trans., ed. and annotated by Frederick Engels (New York: International Publishers, 1948), p. 31.

17. A well-known, if somewhat surprising, exception to this, but only within a system of "concurrent majorities," wherein the democratic principle of majority rule is reasonably maintained while the principle of popular sovereignty is held to be paramount in a democratic order, can be found in John C. Calhoun, *A Disquisition on Government*, ed. by Richard K. Cralle (New York: Peter Smith, 1943), p. 1 and passim. Of course, it always depends on who is invited to the party.

Chapter Seven

A Liberal System Under Assault

Ideology and social myth, which can be usefully understood in a nearly, but not quite, identical manner, become materially manifest. Both are expressions of doctrines that have become largely accepted. Yet while myth, in the sense employed here, is what people honestly think they believe, ideology is what they really believe. The test of myth is testimony; the test of ideology is observable behavior; and while a prevailing myth and a prevailing ideology may be compatible, they often are not. [1]

Within modern political systems the major civic activity in which most people engage, and which is publicly verifiable on an aggregate scale, is voting, and the discrepancies between what people say and how they respond to appeals that finally attract or discourage their vote are frequently notable. To the degree they are being straightforward about what they orally communicate, this strongly suggests that the myth that Americans generally applaud is not the same as their ideology on the basis of which they typically act. In fact, the available data disclose that they reflexively favor democracy as a myth but are liberals, and even conservatives, in their ideological commitments. Furthermore, they are usually unaware that these are fundamentally inconsistent points of view.

* * *

This leads to a particular configuration of power. Those on the "Left" of the rather narrow spectrum of American politics often bemoan the hegemonic position of corporate enterprise; those on the "Right" play to the anger of many who feel themselves to be locked out of the American dream; while the "Center," implicitly or overtly, acclaims economic efficiency and a concurrent equality as historical outcomes of corporate productivity. Then there are the libertarians who, in varying alliances with each side at different times, laud the material and liberty-producing advantages of free enterprise while managing to ignore the very existence of the corporation. Still, whatever the particularity of view, all are eager proponents of democracy even when clucking with disapproval at the mass credulity of the lowest common denominator, which they occasionally perceive to be pandered to by those who are well paid to enhance the rate of corporate profit—in the name, to be sure, of the employees and the stockholders.

These are the throes of an order that encourage an avalanche of cultural analyses, many of which purport to address the lost promise of national purpose. Indeed, such a focus on culture comes to largely replace the study of politics instead of illuminating it because its practitioners generally dismiss the fact that America is a land of many subcultures subsumed within a permeating ideology of liberalism. Accordingly, much is made about a diversity of regions, races, ethnicities, genders, and lifestyles. Yet, as C. Wright Mills succinctly points out, when it comes to public effect only certain kinds of differences are usually applauded in the United States.[2] In fact, the system will intensely resist any attempt to employ policy to enhance instances of countervailing power which cannot be assimilated into the interests of corporate commerce.

The outcome, on one hand, is to applaud and even promote the legitimacy of cultural diversity. On the other, it works to disguise the growing reality of corporate hegemony as the preeminent ideological expression of American values. And, as the material foundations of this phenomenon become more obscure, their manifestations are translated into a widely accepted corporate worldview that, in accord with its liberal roots, substitutes the language of economics for that of political discourse.

Once incredibly revolutionary in releasing a portion of humanity from the bondage of material necessity, a liberal order thus stalls at the boundaries of its own success. For quite some time "liberals have suffered noticeably from a loss of ideological inspiration, a lack of political direction, and an inability to discuss the nation's problems with imagination or creativity."[3] In thrall to their vociferously declared rendition of human limits, they can go no further because they cannot visualize anywhere further to go. All that even the most progressive of American liberals can support is a moderate redistribution of a steadily multiplying pile of material wealth even while they deplore political alienation and the content of popular taste. As a consequence, they ignore the reasons for the enormous concentration of power that causes the ethos which they avidly claim to resist.

Without a doubt, the liberal affection for capitalist efficiency has long been accompanied by a concern for personal liberty. Moreover, for many, this is the ultimate appeal of capitalism. Thus, in compliance with its aversion to power, the liberal tradition consistently asserts that the rights to life and liberty become functional only when they rest upon the foundation of the absence of economic power which supposedly epitomizes a free market and that allows the full enjoyment of the right to property which is crucial to it. Appropriately, a liberal people are not especially bothered by the private wealth of a few, even at those rare moments when they are actually aware of its enormity: in fact, their usual response is to aspire to emulate the rich. But they are deeply troubled by what they perceive as the tyrannical tendencies of those who wield political authority precisely because of their command on productive property.

This is not surprising. For England and, by extension, for much of its empire, liberalism comes as an overlay on a long experience with a variety of regimes and their justifying formulations—an experience that remains generally vivid within the awareness of their populations. Yet to Europeans of the seventeenth and eighteenth centuries the Western hemisphere was virtually a state of nature. For the liberals of the Old World, here were continents devoid of inhabitants and, accordingly, a history. Or, as Locke himself put it, "once all the world was America," and, from the late-seventeenth century on, much of North America was subject to invasion by waves of English immigrants who increasingly arrived with the Lockean contract in their heads.

The result, as Louis Hartz contends, is that what will become the United States is soon engulfed by a liberal ideology without the mitigation that knowledge of a different systemic past has the effect of imposing.[4] In a land born anew all are liberals regardless of where they came from; the dynastic tradition of the Puritans is soon perceived as an archaic conservative remnant that enlightened thought is in the process of discarding; while more democratic claims are overwhelmed by the expansive opportunities for the main chance as seen by people subsumed into the capitalist promise of material accumulation and personal wealth. The consequence is a country that is rapidly and profoundly conditioned to an emerging culture of liberalism. Indeed, the essential wisdom of liberal doctrine becomes compelling and effectively unquestioned in the United States precisely because it meets little ideological resistance—a reality that impedes its ability to respond to its own contradictions and the emergence of a combination of populism with corporate conservatism.

* * *

This is an outlook which infuses a country that endlessly lauds individualism. Its inhabitants accordingly worry a great deal about whether an issue is truly public or private and, when determined to be beyond the capacity of individuals or even private organizations to deal with and, therefore, to be a public matter, about what collectivity, or level of government, should be awarded jurisdiction. Such is a perspective that habitually elevates the private over the public and, when public action is reluctantly found to be required, favors the most decentralized authority deemed capable of addressing the problem. What this actually reveals is not democracy, but a reflexive liberal distrust of authority that, within the current parlance of American politics, is strangely portrayed as conservative, a posture that claims to applaud individualism and despise conformity—except, to be sure, that imposed by the controlling laws of economics.

In any event it is quite understandable that at-large elections for the House of Representatives, or for state legislatures, although not prohibited by the Constitution have, at least since the late-eighteenth century, seldom been entertained as serious options in the United States. Or that the basis of representation of state sovereignty in the United States Senate cannot be changed by the amending procedures in Article V of the Constitution short of unanimous agreement by a three-quarters vote of every state legislature. For this version of conservatism, small becomes the essence of the democratic experience in America: an alleged echo of the Jeffersonian preference for local supremacy.

However, Jefferson might have noticed that the present acclaim for localism in the public realm of government, has become allied with a relentless momentum toward consolidation in the private realm of economics, and that this is not a development which supports even the liberal idea of individualism, to say nothing of the more egalitarian view of the human possibilities. It is also unlikely that he would have missed the point that a centralization of political authority is what a real conservative position always promotes—as well as the role of those corporate interests that simultaneously finance and benefit from its ideological acceptance—phenomena which are not very local in their major tendencies. Still, such conservatives rarely apply their suspicions about government to business corporations. Even fewer attribute corporate power to the logic of the liberal market itself and its definition of opportunity as pecuniary ambition.

In such a manner, confusion about conservatism becomes rampant. But this has little to do with an actual conservative outlook. What the situation truly entails is a pervasive conflict between the liberal proponents of an expansionist capital formation and the residual inclinations of a democratic affectation for small government. Those who speak for each of these doctrinal outlooks steadily bolster the popular conviction that the United States is an egalitarian country and that they epitomize the best possibilities of its continuation. Nevertheless, the patent reality is the erosion of local authority. As the clan replaced small horde-like groups of hunters and gatherers, and the tribe replaced the clan, and the nation-state replaced the tribe, the nation-state now enters the process of surrendering to a transnational order of capital accumulation characterized by enormous investments and worldwide influence all of which are pervading expressions of the conservative Enlightenment.

Indeed, it is evident that a presiding commitment to greater productivity and the bottom line long ago surpassed the rationale for free markets, and that the corporate order represents a social movement that emanates less from business conspiracies than from the rational demands of industrial and post-industrial economics. The corporation becomes dominant simply because it is more efficient in production, sales, distribution, and maintenance than smaller business entities—except, as John Steinbeck notes, when it attempts to fabricate things that demand intense and persistent creative effort. Plainly, "where it has entered such fields, it has succeeded only in adulterating the product and eventually destroying the producer."[5]

Nevertheless, propelled by an adherence to productive efficiency and ever-expanding rates of profit, and by the fact that no capitalist will tolerate price competition any longer than they must,[6] a little noticed corporate revolution—or counterrevolution—replaces the invisible hand. Market values are transmuted into support for a plutocracy of finance, and the great business enterprise increasingly looms as a primary social institution and the paramount locus of publicly effective power. Within this arrangement, anyone who truly matters is, strangely, at least an incipient entrepreneur; people do not identify with labor if they can possibly help it; and citizens are transformed into subjects whose primary civic obligation is to consume. Rule should be exercised by those who are capable of it, and to check their authority with those who are less qualified is ridiculous. Such is a scenario wherein constitutional government becomes the guardian of corporate rights and the loyal promoter of the me-first society.

* * *

Thus do the great hopes of the far-left wing of the European Enlightenment for a more egalitarian world now appear to be dashed upon the jagged shoals of economic reason. Nevertheless, political sensibilities seem to expand, and those disposed to the self-satisfaction of elitist formulations feel pressured by many who are suddenly able to legitimately resist the entrenched claims of family affiliation and privilege. The expected configuration of labor versus capital apparently dissolves as greater quantities of goods and services are dispatched to a populace which toils during the day only to anxiously search out the latest fluctuations of its stock portfolios at night. Majorities are lauded even as they become more irrelevant to power, while those who presumably rule in their name are often portrayed as being nowhere in particular or, perhaps, dispersed into a uniquely liberal panorama of a pressure-group pluralism. The restraints on authority that exemplify an entrepreneurial order are absorbed into the "organizational irresponsibility"[7] of a managerial stratum enriching itself—a development that is largely opaque to a population entranced by the technological artifacts this panorama so abundantly produces and glaringly advertises.

This is a strange twist on the dream of reason—a milieu wherein the basis of the hegemonic power which is allegedly under assault is eagerly applauded by those who are traditionally perceived to be the catalyst of this assault. To be sure, what intrudes upon some is a vaguely defined sense of disaffection with the system and, perhaps at moments, a growing unease about the official definition of the people. But within a constellation of a controlling conformity, these are voices that are barely heard and, when they are, which find little audience capable of moving toward a more egalitarian outcome.

It is, of course, conceivable that all of this may simply express a necessary material progression which eventuates in the kind of highly technocratic order graphically portrayed in works such as *Brave New World:* [8] an order wherein a prevailing adherence to efficiency incessantly erodes any remnant of liberal concerns about the protection of the individual against the reach of the state. Still, private money can yield public authority for only so long as a substantial portion of the population pays deference to the rich, and while resistance to this deeply ingrained cultural habit is effectively consigned to the margins of the order.

NOTES

1. Cf., H. Mark Roelofs, *Ideology and Myth in American Politics: A Critique of a National Political Mind* (Boston: Little, Brown and Co., 1976), p. 4 and passim, and chap. 1, "Critical Knowledge in Politics," pp. 1–5, and, in particular, "Ideology and Myth," pp. 32–45.

2. Mills, *Power Elite*, chap. 1, "The Higher Circles," pp. 3–29, especially, pp. 3–27.

3. Richard H. Pells, *The Liberal Mind in a Conservative Age: American Intellectuals in the 1940s and 1950s*, 2nd. ed. with a new intro. (Hanover, NH: Wesleyan University Press, 1989), p. xviii.

4. Hartz, *Liberal Tradition in America*, cited supra, chap. 1, n. 10.

5. John Steinbeck, *America and Americans: And Selected Nonfiction*, ed. by Susan Shillinglaw and Jackson J. Benson (New York: Viking, 2002), chap. 8, "America and Americans," pp. 313–402, and, especially, p. 358.

6. Cf., Edward Hallett Carr, no. 2, "From Competition to Planned Economy," in Edward Hallett Carr, *The New Society* (New York: St Martin's Press/Macmillan, 1965), pp. 19–39, and, in particular, pp. 23–26.

7. Mills, *White Collar*, p. 149.

8. Cf., Aldous Huxley, *Brave New World* (New York and London: Harper and Brothers, 1946).

Chapter Eight

The American Version of Corporatism

Residing on these margins are those who perceive corporate power as leading to an American version of fascism. And this is a matter which introduces traditional and largely discarded formulations about the content and texture of the national character and how, under postindustrial circumstances, these might play out within a global arena. But, more importantly, it also involves those Romantic epistemological assumptions which inform the centrality of feeling and will in a Fascist culture, and here the rational basis of liberal economics as an expression of the Enlightenment cannot be avoided, as can the logic that leads to a rational corporate system. Nonetheless, at what point corporate power yields an engulfing reign of corporatism which will destroy the individual liberty that supposedly emanates from the pluralistic spillover of government by competing propertied elites may well be the most critical issue that a deeply liberal people presently confront.

Comparing the experience of the United States to the ideological tensions associated with socialism in Europe, and inferring that their absence has saved the country from the unfortunate effects of social-class struggle, most contemporary advocates of liberalism contend that America is unique in human history for having devised an arrangement of equal opportunity that works better for everyone who is willing to take part. This is a mentality which insists that people are economic beings endlessly motivated—and now, maybe, entertained—by the promise of further material consumption within a world of unresolvable scarcity.

It should be noted, however, that a culture which proclaims that the human demand for ever more material consumption is natural, endless, and always at the highest level of intensity has to actually ensure that scarcity or, perhaps more accurately, the perception of scarcity, is permanent. This is a necessity that far exceeds the established understandings of "success" and "failure," of what has been depicted as the lure of wealth and the fear of poverty,[1] as the prime motivations of the order. Those who speak for the status quo find it difficult to face the fact that a capitalist nation, wherein an entrepreneurial ambition for market power is automatically frustrated by the presence of price competitors, is now overwhelmed by an absence of price competition and the market power of the very corporate sector which produces an increasingly available plenitude.

Yet the issue is far more complicated than money. The intractable fact of abundance in postindustrial societies is pivotal to the power relationships that define them—a fact that becomes more pressing as the wealth they yield becomes more visible to people in general. In short, the maintenance of the system makes it increasingly necessary to justify glaringly unequal distributions of income. This now emerges as urgent precisely as it becomes more difficult to successfully hide a rapidly magnifying affluence. The spending policies of corporate business and the state must accord with this necessity. Plainly, acceptable waste, especially through military spending, can be expected to be a major characteristic of such an order. But, most crucially, the foundation of economic policy depends on the myths of the free market, equal opportunity, and earning as natural justifications for the distribution of the wealth. A classical tension between the labor theory of value and the right to profit as the basis of capitalism abounds.

The social and political consequences of this are enormous and hypocritical. They infuse a population which comes to habitually conceive of opportunity as employment by large organized entities—an ever-greater segment of those in the labor force who, if they are to be useful to those who pay them must make the ambitions of the organization their own. What results is not a market-induced liberty but the "corporation man," whose existence is typified by "making motions designed by the minds of others,"[2] and whose most compelling loyalties are to a legal fiction, the corporation itself—absolute necessities for those who would be successful within the structure of a postindustrial world.

* * *

To be sure, any social system demands conformity to the presiding agreements that create it and hold it together—a fact, along with its internal contradictions, which assures that every society is generically corporatist. In this sense, the only option to corporatism is someone's imagination about a state of nature. However, in its more common meaning, corporatism represents the centralizing tendencies of a highly rationalized economic order and its roots in productive techniques that demand an increasingly specialized social division of labor. Hence, in its most acceptable formulation, corporatism advocates a technocratic sharing of political authority by big business, large unions, and government. Despite the present decline of unionism, it is at the core of what is often referred to as industrial policy. In this sense, corporatism is precisely an expression of the probabilities of how people will generally act in light of their present understandings of the economic actualities that impinge upon their existence.

But from a liberal perspective the true inclinations of corporatism are far more insidious. What they connote is the attempt to attain an ersatz equality through the assimilation of the individual into the conformist purposes of the state and, in more progressive interpretations, the state as it serves large financial interests. Still, by either definition, corporatism—and the reaction against it—are each catapulted into existence by liberalism itself. It can thus be considered a force of history—not as a phenomenon which is beyond the control of human beings, but as the aggregate effects of choices made by critical masses of populations in response to their perceptions of their own material situation. [3]

Clearly, the most glaring features of any contemporary liberal system are corporatized. They are typified by a bureaucratic configuration of rationally coordinated groups of specialists in invention, design, production, allocation, law, finance, training, sales, advertising, public relations, and organization itself. Such is a stratum within large commercial entities which John Kenneth Galbraith refers to as the technostructure, an arrangement of functions exemplified not by adventurous entrepreneurial personalities beholden only to the market, but by the group think of employees who are willing to comply with the purposes not their own. And it is here, he argues, where the power that drives major business decisions is found—decisions that are effectively ratified by managers who are themselves enmeshed within a complex constellation of organized expertise which they hire yet hardly comprehend. Corporate policy is then announced by, and attributed to, those who officially speak for companies that, increasingly, are legally owned by stockholders who grasp or, usually, care, even less than the managers about the actual operations of the firm. These imperatives, as Galbraith points out, also apply to government. What accordingly emerges is an operational fusion of "private" and "public" technostructures. [4]

Such is a bureaucratic order to which Max Weber reluctantly warned the rationalism of the Enlightenment would lead. [5] Certainly, this is not a liberal world as most liberals define it. But the concentration of economic power in America, as well as the quasi-diffusion of civic power within and among a range of technostructures, [6] ultimately reflects the logic of the commodity consciousness which a liberal ideology promotes. To be sure, as Thorstein Veblen asserts, sabotaging production often yields enhanced profit rates. [7] Still, this remains a system which extols and supports the primacy of the material largess that emanates from productive efficiency allegedly motivated by entrepreneurial competition and the right to profit—values that, in America, are so engrained they are seemingly natural and beyond dispute.

The consequence is an incessant concern with the bottom line and an unremitting struggle for greater market share within a panorama of affluence—a competition for prestige and privilege among bureaucratic structures that often leads to an arrogant sense of entitlement or, at times, to that which resembles a claim to royal prerogative predicated upon the presumption of a rational superiority.

To the extent that these values suffuse all others they must be interlocked with and supported by government, since that which is perceived to be most efficient must authoritatively prevail. Yet the traditional liberal anxiety about unrestrained authority does not seem to apply to this condition. And it is exactly in this manner that Hobbes' Leviathan[8] looms as a distinct possibility—a corporatist megastate[9] that will wipe out all traces of a liberal individualism, and wherein all who are citizens directly or indirectly are employed by the company.

* * *

"Mechanized and standardized work, the decline of any chance for the employee to see and understand the whole operation, the loss of any chance, save for the very few, for private contact with those in authority"[10]—these are the mandates of a rational division of labor, mandates which equally assimilate those independent entrepreneurs who provide services for major corporations along with their suppliers and customers. This requires a process of acculturation which Galbraith depicts as identification and which is implicit within organizations of any kind, large or small, and whether they are public or private. Following this, Galbraith argues, once a respectable organizational position is secured, an attempt to influence the goals of the operation, is likely to occur.[11]

But, within the culture of commerce which this version of Enlightenment yields, adaptive behavior is severely circumscribed by the need to assure the financial security of the enterprise: a demand that can never be ignored. For business corporations this supposedly means a ceaseless preoccupation with profitability. Nevertheless, within the major pecuniary enterprises of the modern age of corporatism, an adherence to the bottom line comes to be accompanied by a pressing concern with the size of the company relative to others—most specifically to those which—at least vaguely—are in the same field of endeavor. For those who populate corporate circles, a commitment to a greater rate of profit now frequently competes with a desire for the status that accrues to the comparative position of those who attain a larger market share, even at the cost of a lower rate of return on dollars invested. This is to impress not only the larger public but, perhaps more cogently, their corporate compatriots. It follows that what mergers, acquisitions, and buyouts often express is not a hunger for more lucre but a need for power—a need that becomes more insistent once a certain level of personal affluence can be reasonably assumed. Herein lurk the tendencies of the liberal Enlightenment toward a conservative corporatism and, perhaps, even the anomaly of a rational fascism.

That power is finally a more profound motivation than money is well illustrated by behavior which actually reduces the overall income of a business. There is, for instance, the establishment of foundations by rich institutions or individuals. Or by the financing or self-financing of political campaigns; or, in a more mundane sense, by corporate or personal investments in major sports franchises; or even, in a somewhat less newsworthy fashion, the ability to purchase large blocs of the best tickets. Regardless of the possible tax and policy advantages, seldom does any of this reflect a rational pursuit of wealth—although the pervasive influence of cultural lag[12] assures that public discussion about it is generally couched in these terms. What it represents is an attempt to gain the status and esteem that flows even from the much-publicized financial losses that may be incurred, and the public respect and influence this kind of behavior commands.

Within the corporation itself there are, of course, more systemic reasons for not maximizing profit margins. Those who already identify with the company generally want to expand its size in order to employ more people, hence, among other things, creating layers of personnel with less seniority in the firm as a buffer in the event of layoffs.[13] And, if a periodic reversion to the primacy of the bottom line results in such a tactic not always working out as planned, this does not deny the intention of many within the enterprise to follow a policy of growth and, thereby, status and, ultimately, power at the expense of profit rates. Then there is always the residual presence of what Veblen labels "the instinct of workmanship" which, to varying degrees among different people, is in conflict with "predatory" behavior, "pecuniary prowess," and "the instinct for emulation" as displays of the exploitive "success" which, for Veblen, are much admired during the "barbaric" and "business" stages of history.[14] Or, in a more acceptable American lexicon, a need for workmanship is always opposed to those pecuniary manipulations which infuse the liberal version of equal opportunity.

In a more profound sense, however, the desire to maximize the magnitude of the modern corporation and, thereby, corporatism itself, testifies to a distorted residue of a liberal ideology within an order where price-competitive activities are found, if at all, only on its fringes and, most often, at its underground edges. Hence, the language and habits of capitalism continue to permeate a system within which free markets rarely, if ever, exist, a view largely carried forward by the immigrant history of the nation. Thus the entrepreneurial individual is acclaimed but team players are wanted, and undue efforts to enhance the rate of profit through too much competitive risk, which might comprise a threat to the integrity of the organization, are discouraged. In fact, as corporate accumulation proceeds, the pursuit of greater profit margins persistently accedes to a quest for power in the guise of economics.

* * *

These tendencies are abundantly expressed in the presiding patterns of fiscal policy in the United States during much of the past century. To ground a claim to privilege upon the assertion of a right is, of course, the linguistic coin of the realm in a liberal nation. And over the years such rights have expanded into many new arenas of societal existence, encouraging governmental spending that has augmented the general level of incomes to an extent which would have been branded as un-American not too long ago. Despite its downward effect on immediate profit rates through taxation, and regardless of their own rhetoric, it has occurred to more than a few within corporate America that this is good for business. It patently supports the stabilizing requirements of the economic system by buying off large-scale monetary discontent in the face of a rapidly growing productive capacity and output that has reached public perception. But, most significantly, a more equitable allocation of the wealth creates employment and, thereby, the totality of effective demand.

Such an emphasis on economic rights also equalizes civic power, at least to a minor extent. Yet even progressive liberals are steeped in a free-market ideology which typically prevents them from fully appreciating the consolidating imperatives of the technological basis of the order; as well as their cultural ramifications; and the patterns of public policy which must result. Presumably critical of values that are, at bottom, financial, they usually ignore the point that the idea of productive property possessing rights is nothing but a legal fiction that is fundamental to what they presumably oppose. And, while they sometimes recognize human needs that exceed economics, and which are essentially civilizing in their inherent tendencies, they lack any cogent analysis of why the fulfillment of these needs is severely circumscribed by the conceptions of reason and human nature which critically inform their own viewpoint. Clearly, if things are wrong someone must be at fault, and much of the energy of the "Left" is devoted to denigrating the bad guys and looking for the good guys—a posture which avoids any serious attempt to comprehend the actual content of a liberal culture becoming more conservative wherein people are saturated with certain notions of appropriate behavior that flow from a market version of the Enlightenment. This renders it difficult for them to even tolerate the idea that scarcity might be abolished and, hence, what the prospect of material abundance could mean for American politics.

* * *

As Lincoln Steffens long ago noted, liberal reform movements, even when they apparently attain early success, predictably revert to a new—and usually less competent—version of the status-quo ante.[15] That is, in a country where the ideology of liberalism is supreme, the cultural truths that drive the order are simply untouched by reform. Plainly, many who adhere to a more progressive brand of liberalism are not resistant to moderate steps toward greater income equality by adjusting distribution while leaving production alone, thereby priming the pump through easy credit, low interest rates, and the appropriate taxation, spending, and regulatory policies of the state. But if by reform is meant that which moves toward a further equality of power and authority, they too stand in strident opposition to any serious effort to transform what is a very stable political arrangement. As a consequence, an inability to articulate an actual democratic perspective pervades: a perspective that is not about property rights, or even material condition or result, but about a more egalitarian distribution of civic power and which, subtly or overtly, is characteristically dismissed as unrealistic and naive.

Of course, some more egalitarian policies have attained a degree of shaky permanence. Yet these involved more than reform. Much as Jefferson wanted to increase the public influence of individual farmers who, at that time, comprised the majority of the white male inhabitants of British North America, so the New Deal and its extension in the 1960s encouraged the countervailing power of a wide range of groups which were devoid of substantial productive property holdings—a position that was, and still is, subversive to those who continue to cling to a laissez-faire liberalism. Thus, if the Jeffersonians represented a managed rebellion, the inclination of these more recent movements to civilize capitalism when business could not were actually less efforts to reform the system than attempts to bring about a limited revolution within it.

In any event, the dynamics of contradiction will not remain quiet, and it is within these that the transitions of cultural commitments always find their roots. The liberal revolution radiated from the dialectical tensions which infused the technological foundations of the dynastic systems of Western Europe. This is a revolution that now intrudes into many other regions of the globe even as it is confronted by a more egalitarian ethos which ramifies from the paradoxes that inform the corporatist core of a postcapitalist order. The outcome is a confusing cacophony of liberal democracy and scientific technology as a world-historical force, a force wherein a more democratic revolution insistently rides the back of an earlier and still-expanding revolution of the reason of the Enlightenment hidden within an elitism of commerce.

NOTES

1. Cf., Paul M. Sweezy, *The Theory of Capitalist Development: Principles of Marxian Political Economy* (New York: Monthly Review Press, 1956).

2. Erich Fromm, *The Sane Society* (New York: Rinehart and Co., 1955), p. 223.

3. For a useful analysis of this, cf., Robert L. Heilbroner, *The Future as History: The Historic Currents of Our Time and the Direction in Which They Are Taking America* (New York: Harper and Brothers, 1960), chap. 1, "The Encounter with History," pp. 1–8, and, in particular, pp. 28–30.

4. For this controversial interpretation of the corporate system, cf., John Kenneth Galbraith, *The New Industrial State* (Boston: Houghton Mifflin Co., 1967), on "The Technostructure," p. 71 and passim, capitalized for emphasis in the original in its first usage, and, especially, chap. 6, "The Technostructure," pp. 60–71, and chap. 8, "The Entrepreneur and the Technostructure," pp. 86–97.

5. As suggested in Max Weber, *The Theory of Social and Economic Organization*, ed. with an intro. by Talcott Parsons, trans. by A. M. Henderson and Talcott Parsons, The Falcon's Wing Press (Glencoe, IL: The Free Press, 1947), p. 146 and passim. Also, ibid, II., "Legal Authority with a Bureaucratic Administrative Staff," 3: "Legal authority: The Pure Type with Employment of a Bureaucratic Administrative Staff," pp. 329–41.

6. Cf., for instance, Galbraith, *New Industrial State*, chap. 25, "The Educational and Scientific Estate," pp. 282–95 and passim, and chap. 35, "The Future of the Industrial State," pp. 388–99.

7. Cf., Thorstein Veblen, especially chap. 1, "On the Nature and Uses of Sabotage," in Thorstein Veblen, *The Engineers and the Price System*, Reprints of Economic Classics (New York: Augustus M. Kelley, Bookseller, 1965), pp. 21–26.

8. Thomas Hobbes, *Leviathan*, with an intro. by A. D. Lindsay, Everyman's Library (New York: E. P. Dutton and Co., 1950).

9. Sheldon S. Wolin, in Sheldon S. Wolin, *The Presence of the Past: Essays on the State and the Constitution*, The John Hopkins Series in Constitutional Thought, ed. by Sotirios Barber and Jeffrey Tulis (Baltimore: The Johns Hopkins University Press, 1989), p. 183 and passim, and, more generally, no. 10, "Democracy without the Citizen," pp. 180–91, and no. 11, "Democracy and Operation Democracy," pp. 192–207.

10. Mills, *White Collar*, p. 212.

11. Cf., Galbraith, *New Industrial State*, in particular, chap. 13, "Motivation and the Technostructure," pp. 149–58. Also cf., Herbert A. Simon, *Administrative Behavior: A Study of Decision-Making Processes in Administrative Organization*, with a foreword by Chester I. Barnard (New York: The Macmillan Co., 1948), chap. 10, "Loyalties and Organizational Identification," pp. 198–219.

12. Thorstein Veblen, *The Instinct of Workmanship and the State of the Industrial Arts*, with an intro. by Dr. Joseph Dorfman (New York: Augustus M. Kelley, Bookseller, 1964), p. 27 and passim, quoted for emphasis in the original in its first usage, and, more generally, chap. 1, "The Instinct of Workmanship: Introductory," pp. 1–37, and Thorstein Veblen, *The Theory of the Leisure Class: An Economic Study of Institutions*, with a foreword by Stuart Chase, The Modern Library (New York: Random House, 1934), p. 33 and passim.

13. Cf., Galbraith, *New Industrial State*, chap. 15, "The Goals of the Industrial System," pp. 166–78, and, especially, pp. 171–72.

14. Veblen, *Theory of the Leisure Class*.

15. Lincoln Steffens, *The Autobiography of Lincoln Steffens*, complete in one volume, illustrated (New York: Harcourt, Brace and Co., 1931, and, in particular, Part 3, "Muckraking," pp. 355–627, art 4, "Revolution," pp. 629–837, and Part 5, "Seeing America at Last," pp. 839–73.

Chapter Nine

Pluralism, the Enlightenment, and Science

If those who argue that the development of the human brain has allowed people to largely escape what is instinctive and to increasingly ground their existence in what would have to be considered actual choices are correct, then it is clear that humanity enters the realm of the political as a fundamental consequence of free will.

Yet, not quite so simply. "Men," as Marx tells us, "make their own history, but they do not make it just as they please; they do not make it under circumstances chosen by themselves, but under circumstances directly encountered, given, and transmitted from the past." While all animals are embedded in instinct, the human animal is also embedded in culture, and in that presiding ideology through which culture is articulated. It is thus that "the tradition of all the dead generations weighs like a nightmare on the brain of the living."[1]

* * *

What exactly comprises a culture is notably debatable. Here, however, the intent is to arrive at a universal conception that may be operationally useful to political inquiry within a condition of modernity. In this, C. P. Snow is instructive when he suggests that those who share a culture exhibit common responses to the same stimuli, inferring that a culture is nothing more than a constellation of agreements among certain people about what is real and what is important.[2] As such it introduces a panorama of values as well as attitudes—which are values that people actually hold but of which they are not fully aware—that result in these agreements. Accordingly, by its very character, a culture must be ethnocentric or, to employ what, unfortunately, has become a pejorative term, an inherently reductionist phenomenon. This is because any culture is invariably limited and, indeed, defined, by its agreed-upon view of the nature of the universe, society, and the species which it expresses.

On the basis of such an approach, the evidence indicates that human beings are actually members of a variety of cultures, some of which they share only with certain people and some strictly with others, whether they live in territorial proximity or not. Hence a person might respond in a similar way to a particular stimulus as do some people scattered throughout the world—a stimulus to which their immediate neighbors might respond to quite differently, or not at all—even while they and their neighbors will probably react in a common manner to a great range of other stimuli, reactions which those residing elsewhere may or may not share.

Many anthropologists would, undoubtedly, object to this formulation because it eliminates the necessity of a contiguous population as a factor whereby a culture is understood. But this is precisely the point. Its effect is to vastly pluralize the very notion of cultural commitments, suggesting a distinction between and among cultures confined to specific regions and those which are not; or, maybe, between cultures and subcultures; or, of more direct concern to political analysis, between cultures that are locally hegemonic and those which may be comparatively limited in membership yet even global in influence. Each of these reflects and affects human behavior and, accordingly, the substance of power and power relationships. They thus become material elements of the human situation, and, while varying in intensity and duration, significant to any effort to understand the political ramifications of the Enlightenment.

* * *

Sociologists typically conceive of a human group as two or more persons between or among whom there is frequent and regular interaction. Such groups are considered to be primary when these interactions are typically face-to-face and secondary when they are not. Groups which perceive a common interest become interest groups, and interest groups that organize to pursue their perceived interests through influencing public policy are held to be pressure groups or, as some prefer, special interest groups.

Accepting the inference of Harold D. Lasswell and Abraham Kaplan that "a social order"[3] is a group with its culture, it follows that people who interact on a frequent and regular basis, either in a primary or secondary fashion, or more predictably, in both, and who share common responses to the same stimuli, constitute a society. In short, regularized interactions among human beings transform cultures into societies and makes their participants into members of an array of societies, some of which they share with certain people and some only with others, irrespective of their geographic location.

Some of these agreements are national in scope. Thus the common responses of people to the same stimuli express a cultural consensus that, when accompanied by their frequent and regular interactions, comprises the content and distribution of power and authority by which a national society is delineated. Yet within this exists a diversity of societies that literally become political systems in themselves. While these generally function within the nation, they become especially crucial to power and authority when tensions emerge between a commitment to the nation-state as a society and loyalties to societies that are transnational, such as those of corporate capital and modern science, both of which are worldwide in their reach.

* * *

In a country too vast and complex for rule by majorities, all of this must lead the argument for political equality to a focus on pluralism, a formulation that gains intellectual credibility in the first third of the twentieth century when it is put forward by the realist critics of a traditional emphasis on the institutions of government as the proper approach to political analysis. Emphasizing "informal" as distinct from "formal" factors as the basis of inquiry, the pluralist outlook contends that the fundamental fact of social existence is the affiliation of human beings with a range of identifiable groups. In so doing, it also redefines the liberal notion of the possessive individual,[4] and power itself, into a group phenomenon, a perspective which effectively challenges the traditional Madisonian aversion to "factions" by elevating them to a new and, indeed, positive status.[5]

Civic action always involves organization, whether overt, implicit or, as is typically the case, both. On this basis, "group theory" claims to be far more useful to grasping the actualities of political existence than approaches which emphasize individuals or even majorities. Of course, people find connection with many groups and personal tension often results when these "overlapping memberships"[6] in various societies come into conflict over specific issues. However, the pluralist contention invariably implies that these dynamics are limited by larger agreements that compose the dominant system and which, in the modern world, is generally the nation-state. Thus, within any system purported to be pluralistic—and all systems presumably are—acceptable action must conform to a controlling ideology to which the members of every group are acculturated. This comprises the public interest.

In short, pluralism is not a system. The fact is that the system must exist before pluralism can even become a consideration because it is this which establishes the boundaries wherein differences between and among competing interests are played out and, in reality as opposed to appearance, it is in the interest of every group to maintain. These are often alleged to be the "rules of the game"—and which, when applied to the United States, constitute "the democratic mold"[7]—or, more accurately, an adherence to those delegations of and constraints on political authority enunciated by the Constitution. And, at least for the prevailing portrayal of American pluralism, they are rules that notably imitate the competitive stipulations of the free market.[8] Hence group dynamics are presumably contained by a commitment to the implicit principles of a presiding contract that flows from the liberal Enlightenment, and which, in this instance, are themselves pluralistic.

On the other hand, many who champion a greater political equality, while being critical of those who celebrate pluralism as "democracy," too easily dismiss the possibilities of pluralism as little more than the antimajoritarian clashes and alliances of moneyed elites within an arena of "pressure-group politics."[9] This may be an accurate evaluation of what currently characterizes the power system in America. Yet it also represents a perceptual rigidity that allows its advocates to ignore the issues of why the rules that control the system are what they are, an issue that any proponent of a more democratic order must address. What they might notice is that the pluralist outlook is frequently predicated upon a series of if-then propositions, yielding what are really logical constructions, not theories: that is, pluralists usually state and describe but make no serious attempt to search for the causalities of what they are portraying.[10]

As a consequence, the argument stipulates the existence of a political arena that somehow emerged—a configuration wherein the players change but which is itself devoid of change, and wherein the only possible motion is that which occurs within the confines of what is already established. In this manner, form is lauded while any consideration of historical process is avoided. This encourages a perspective within which all developments regarding consciousness and ideology are ignored and which only recognizes an already-existing order of power and authority that, in the American instance, apparently began with the formulation of the social contract.

To be sure, some proponents of pluralism do state, describe, and attempt to explain relationships; support this with empirically verifiable evidence; and forecast and even predict behavior within the system. To this degree pluralism is useful as a theory. But it is a theory of a second order of explanatory power. It is too circumscribed to be a social theory since it exhibits no notable interest in the problem of how the rules of the game emerged. Instead, insofar as its advocates simply assume the existence of the order as a self-evident premise, it resembles systems analysis and structural functionalism, both of which are variations on the theme of pluralism. As such, the accepted idea of pluralism in the United States inferentially denies the feasibility of further human development and the probable influence of such development on the ideology through which a dominant culture becomes manifest—phenomena which must suggest an often discomforting possibility of social revolution. The result is to transform "democracy" into a range of "active minorities"[11] that compete with, cooperate with, or ignore others like themselves, depending on the issue. These reflect a variety of perceived interests—an alleged array of contending leaders which increasingly becomes a surrogate for majorities.

* * *

Plainly, the diverse loci of authority that epitomizes a pluralistic order and the concentration of authority in a majority demanded by the democratic argument are incompatible propositions. Moreover, many democrats would suspect the presence of interests that exceed the limits of the system. It is also evident that the doctrine from which the ideology of pluralism derives is riddled with questionable abstractions, although people sufficiently conditioned to a culture of liberal economics consider them to be only realistic and finally common sense. Nevertheless, notions of private as distinct from public wealth, the rights not only to, but of, property, a free market, equal opportunity, and an insistent preoccupation with an irresolvable material scarcity in the midst of a multiplying abundance are not common sense in terms of any empirical analysis of the needs and aspirations that infuse the politics of modernity. In fact, the liberal portrayal of people as insatiable economic animals, while revolutionary in the epoch of its initial formulation becomes, within an era of monumental productivity, rather shallow, and even somewhat primitive, in its essential claims about human nature. Still, those who are conditioned to a monolithically liberal country are unlikely to know any other vocabulary than that of laissez-faire. In America, this becomes central to the pluralist position itself.

Accordingly, liberal pluralists resist the notion that there is any conceivable replacement for their abiding commitment to a diversity of power restricted by market forces that eventuate in rule by a stratum of competing propertied elites—a perception that continues to prevail despite the actualities of an order within which price-competitive markets seldom exist, and then not for long. In brief, a more democratic system is not only undesirable, it is not feasible. So Madison makes the argument,[12] as do most contemporary American pluralists, although many of them apparently feel obliged to pay tribute to democracy with some kind of hyphenated term that ends with "democracy"[13] even while assuring that majorities do not govern.

It follows that the much-repeated bromide that capitalist economics will lead to a democratic balance of power and authority is at the core of the pluralist formulation in United States. Hence, its devotees implicitly insist on applying the assumptions of laissez-faire to the centralizing facts of a postindustrial epoch that more and more approximates the very mercantilism against which an incipient liberalism of the seventeenth and eighteenth centuries revolted, first in England and then, rather persistently, throughout other portions of the globe. Yet that the vastness of the order prevents majorities from getting in touch with the information necessary to intelligent public decisions is a patent reality. And, even when majorities are broken down into smaller and more empirically observable interest and pressure groups, the issue remains one of whether the country is moving toward a more pluralistic equality of public influence or into the ersatz equality of the consumer society and a monolithic sameness which might provide the seedbed for an American style of fascism—a condition within which money may appear to control social existence but where, in fact, technology does. In short, the standard pluralist argument avoids any attempt to deal with the historical forces which a systemic theory demands. It thus ignores the possible connections between such forces and a challenge to the pervading ideology of corporate power that might result in a more egalitarian pluralism.

* * *

In brief, the theory of pluralism is an excellent attempt to understand the shifting conflicts and alliances that compose what is comprehended as the tangle of organized and yet to be organized political interests. Nevertheless, however diverse the pluralistic struggle for power, it is always confined by those ideological agreements which hold the political arena together, and here some attention to the movement of history is central to understanding the core values of a society that are the basis of these agreements. The action of pluralism can only take place within a the a-priori set of agreements that created the system and which, thereby, stipulate what is acceptable behavior in pursuit of perceived interests, even to the point of transforming them into law. How these agreements form is a crucial and difficult concern of political theory.

Among the attempts to address this issue, themes of progress as technical advance run through human history. Presumably this is because all species react to their material environment and, at the very least, technology and a consequent expansion through military prowess have often been the keys to material abundance or, more typically, the mitigation of scarcity. Thus, even while the Fascist and Nazi attacks on liberalism were rooted in a Romantic assault on reason, their proponents remained quite enamored of technological achievement. Still, they were openly hostile to the Enlightenment and, thereby, to science. If, as a result, their technical efforts suffered—and they did— this was simply an inadvertent, and generally unacknowledged, side effect of their detestation of empiricism as a rationalist corruption of feeling and will.

The significance of all this for pluralism as a political system vastly exceeds the details of these specific episodes in European history. Certainly, what is actually scientific as distinct from technological is often confusing. Nonetheless, its political implications are inescapable. Here the well-documented differences between German engineers, who generally supported the Nazi government, and the physicists, many of whom resisted it, are instructive.[14] What these epitomized was a clash of worldviews which, due to the augmented importance of each to contemporary economics, becomes increasingly blatant. It is here that the foundation and contradictions of any system which emerges from the Enlightenment are to be found.

* * *

While a plethora of technical innovations continuously flow from the applications of scientific investigation, dramatically releasing people from toil and offering them conveniences they never heard of before—or, sometimes, can even use—the imperatives of modern technology patently move toward economic planning and, thereby, the enhancement of corporate power.[15] This now emerges as the major political expression of the conservative Enlightenment. Moreover, under the mandates of mass production and marketing, the operative processes of technology become inherently authoritarian. They necessitate chains of command and delineated spans of administrative control: in short, they rely on the certainties that presumably result from people doing what they are expected to do. They do not exactly encourage a more pluralistic arrangement of power.

But the history of science is another matter. In any large sense, it is a tale of people not doing what they are supposed to do—an arena of public action often epitomized by the unexpected and, frequently, surprise. It involves an attitude of intellectual rebelliousness—a willingness to conceptually leap from what is presumably known into that which appears to be unknown. As such, it demands an ethos of skepticism and an appreciation of the uncertainties which always inform discoveries about the actualities of a material universe—an ethos that offers no finalities except for the presuppositions and assumptions that control its "angle of approach"[16] and that deeply infuse its methodology and, along with technology, its transformation into a political system in itself. In reference to power and authority, what is pluralistic in America increasingly functions within this system.

* * *

Beyond technology, the centrality of science to pluralism in the contemporary world is the most pivotal result of the Enlightenment as a whole, wherein not the truth, but the search for truth, becomes the fundamental cultural commitment of its adherents. Its emphasis is on quest, not claim, a position which patently involves an admission of ignorance that often weakens its immediate influence. What is finally intolerable to the authoritarian mind is the lack of absolutes, and it is precisely this that characterizes the scientific outlook, an outlook which insists that an open-ended approach to truth must prevail over all other claims; a methodology that is dialectically committed to a near-anarchy of hypothesis and theory and a temporary consensus about evidence; an enterprise that yields only a range of plausibilities and probabilities until predicted events are actually observed and from which only useful inferences, or "warranted assertabilities,"[17] about a presupposed universal reality may be induced.

As these forces become more manifest a reaction must be expected, and what results is a clash which reveals where the societal tensions within an American corporatism currently reside—a propensity inadvertently fueled by the fusion of technological advance with the commercial ambitions of aggregated capital. Indeed, it is precisely this combination which induces the major political question of those parts of the world reached by the Enlightenment as to how far the conditioning of populations into a hegemonic corporatism will extend. Much depends on the values of organized science as a countervailing force, along with the ideological reach of its outlook.

Not surprisingly, as with any factor crucial to production, science now becomes an organized force. It is upon this which technology depends. In this manner the scientific enterprise represents both a material and pluralizing force that can make a claim to the respectability that yields power and authority. And, of central importance, its essential values are pluralistic in themselves. These are values that must infiltrate the corporate domain. What they politically signify is a path to public effect through those intellectual and artistic aspirations upon which the scientific impulse conclusively depends. When embedded within an array of technostructures, these comprise a pluralistic resistance to corporatism: a subtle and opposing perspective within the productive basis of the order.

However advanced their level of sophistication, the presiding productive techniques always comprise a force which determines to what extent an order is authoritarian and to what degree it is conducive to an expanding range of freedom. This is because they fundamentally control the manner in which the universe, society and, crucially, human nature are understood—a phenomenon that is ultimately expressed in the transitions of cultures, societies, and ideologies and, accordingly, in the content and distribution of power and authority. As a consequence, it is within the corporate crux of the modern liberal world where the pluralistic potential of the system is presently found. Its major contradiction yields a diversity of influence that is structural and, it follows, far more essential to significant policy than the pluralism which becomes associated with competing lifestyles and a concern with race, ethnicity, gender, and religion as the social issues with which a liberal America is overwhelmingly preoccupied. Indeed, it is within the material foundation of the system that the more egalitarian possibilities of the radical Enlightenment lurk—a development that can only emerge from the scientific constituent that attends the concrete actualities of politics, and wherein the roots of any effective pluralistic opposition to a technocratic corporatism must reside.

* * *

Working as a paradoxical unity, scientific technology thus leads to a fundamental tension which illuminates those contradictory human tendencies that infuse history. The technobureaucratic demand for predictability and control has to confront its own dependence on the pluralism of those random and, frequently, aesthetic hunches that inform the quest for the presumed symmetries of the universe which inspire scientific inquiry—as well as on the requirement of freedom which attends it.

Hence while private wealth, status, and influence in a liberal order typically gravitate to technical achievement, such achievement is beholden to a scientific establishment which is inherently public in its own values, and that finds the locus of its organization within a nexus of universities, research institutions and, to some extent, business firms themselves. Science can be destroyed but it cannot be absorbed by financial interests. Indeed, to destroy it, as the Fascists and Nazis effectively did by attempting to incorporate science into the will of the state, is to eliminate the basis of corporate power itself.

This creates a contradiction which becomes more central as affluence magnifies and is more generally assumed—a contradiction that pluralizes power within a civilization profoundly rooted in scientific technology as an aggrandizing force of history. It is this which has largely neutralized the capitalist version of economic individualism as well as the required localism of democracy. And it is here that the prevailing issues of a postindustrial age become centrally engaged—a unity of opposites leading toward an engulfing corporatist technocracy and, simultaneously, toward the anticonformist values of a scientific ideology.

It follows that a pivotal, if often implicit, competition over policy emerges within and among the various groups of experts that exemplify a postindustrial order and that compose the stratum of the technostructure—as well as among a range of such technostructures. What this comprises is a pluralism of another kind, a pluralism which reveals that the devotees of "the iron law of oligarchy"[18] are fundamentally wrong. Competition is intrinsic to any organization, whether it is thought of as private or public, although to designate the vast impact of corporate activity as private is nothing less than a tribute to the imagination of classical liberals and a splendid way to avoid the actualities of power in the modern world. It is this which now intrudes on the substance and distribution of publicly effective power within a system of liberal capitalism under conservative assault, thereby setting the parameters of significant debate. The methodology of science always represents the basis of opposition to authoritarian claims, and a progressive pluralism must be rooted in the values of science or, at least, in the struggle for a more scientific civilization. Indeed, beyond the issue of pluralism, it is where the material foundation of the greater struggle for political equality, which is at the core of the radical Enlightenment, must be found.

* * *

Yet science itself cannot be democratic. Clearly, the scientific approach stipulates that all hypotheses and theories are not equal and that their verification or falsification involves substantial agreement by a consensus that constitutes more than a majority of qualified observers. Still, it is worth noting that the final test of a hypothesis, or a theory, or even a law, is grounded in the assumption that while everyone is not equal in their immediate ability to weigh the evidence, they are equal in their innate capacity to perceive it. They are, therefore, qualified to observe that which may work to confirm or deny any assertion about reality. In this manner the interior dialectic of a scientific methodology concurrently encourages individuality, or, perhaps, anarchy, in the matter of formulation and the equivalence of political equality in the matter of demonstration.

Accordingly, "the authority of scientific opinion enforces the teachings of science in general, for the very purpose of fostering their subversion in particular points."[19] This induces a cacophony of speculation as a counterpoint to agreements about the presently acceptable "facts," a tension which inescapably infuses the doing of science.[20] What must result is an attitude of pluralistic tentativeness which has to accompany an openness to any evidence that may support or challenge established claims about the empirical probability or, at least, plausibility, of causality or correspondence—a view that may require continuing experimentation, replication, or comparison. It follows that the predictive, or even explanatory, power of a formulation is one thing, but an event, or a fact, cannot be said to exist until it occurs and is, directly or indirectly, observed, while agreement about perception of it cannot be considered to be permanent.

To be sure, there are those who engage in both science as theory as well as science as application, and whose perspective accordingly shifts with this variation in function—a shift that many have difficulty with because one orientation or the other is usually a dominant trait of the personality involved. Each plainly infuses the modern situation—the controlling context wherein conflicts over major policy occur, and within which the temptation to buy science in order to manage its output can only jeopardize the cultural agreements that yield the power of those who would do the buying.

All of this may seem scientifically mundane. But it is politically vital because it transforms science into an organized proponent, both nationally and globally, of a more egalitarian pluralism. It additionally comprises an extremely public perspective which persistently undermines a culture of privileged and private knowledge that justifies every known version of social-class or elite rule. Curiosity is essentially egalitarian and the enterprise of science and any movement toward democracy are invariably in alliance. Or, as Walter Lippman put it, "when the impulse which overthrows kings and priests and unquestioned creeds becomes self-conscious we call it science. . . . It is self-government."[21]

* * *

The commands of technology and the mandates of science lead to behavior that well precedes the story of the Enlightenment. Indeed, the contradictory propensities of what is now called scientific technology have always proceeded in tandem. Whatever their immediate guise, they constitute a fundamental condition locked in critical struggle with itself—a condition that profoundly influences all other institutions which may flourish and decline during specific epochs of the human experience. What is new since the Age of Reason are the magnitudes of power and people involved and, since the values and attitudes that define a culture and then a society finally derive from their primary productive means, the outcome must be a pervasive tension with which the resulting order is suffused. It follows that the present milieu is one wherein the values of technical expertise; an atavistic preoccupation with an endless increase in the rate of profit; and the need for scientific comprehension all strive to establish the arena wherein the dynamics of pluralistic competition play out.

It is only from within the primary productive forces that rule by the few or the one can be seriously assaulted and upon which a more egalitarian pluralism can find a tangible foundation. Societal agreements which result in a political system and agreements about epistemology, about what is considered to be knowledge and how it is properly attained, are inescapably connected. Here the Enlightenment is crucial. But while people generally admire feats of technology, they are usually not as ready to accept the values or even the discoveries of science. In the long run this may not matter because the evidence of history indicates that populations eventually move toward a scientific comprehension of material reality and incorporate it into their own purposes—a fact which in itself becomes a systemic material reality. Yet in the short run it might matter a great deal to the point where a ramifying corporate commercialism might assure that the long run may not matter at all. Such is an arena wherein the connections of science to pluralism become most problematic and a paramount issue of contemporary political theory.

NOTES

1. Karl Marx, "The Eighteenth Brumaire of Louis Bonaparte," in Part 3, "1848 and After," pp. 21–42, in McLellan (ed.), *Karl Marx: Selected Writings*, p. 300.

2. C. P. Snow, *The Two Cultures and the Scientific Revolution*, The Rede Lecture, 1959 (New York: Cambridge University Press, 1959), and, in particular, pp. 2–3.

3. Lasswell and Kaplan, *Power and Society*, p. 50 and passim, "social order" italicized for emphasis in its first usage.

4. Macpherson, *Political Theory of Possessive Individualism*, p. v and passim, cited supra, chap. 1, n. 4.

5. Among the works that had a major influence on the development of pluralism as a systemic theory within professional political science are Arthur F. Bentley, *The Process of Government*, ed. by Peter H. Odegard, The John Harvard Library, ed. by Bernard Bailyn (Cambridge: Harvard University Press, The Belknap Press, 1967); Robert A. Dahl, *A Preface to Democratic Theory*, Charles R. Walgreen Foundation Lectures (Chicago: The University of Chicago Press, 1956), and, in particular, chap, 1, "Madisonian Democracy," pp. 4–33 and chap. 3, "Polyarchal Democracy," pp. 63–89; Robert A. Dahl, *Who Governs?: Democracy and Power in an American City* (New Haven: Yale University Press, 1961); John Dewey, *The Public and Its Problems: An Essay in Political Inquiry* (Chicago: Gateway Books, 1946); Earl Latham, "The Group Basis of Politics: Notes for a Theory," *The American Political Science Review*, June 1952, pp. 376–97; Earl Latham, *The Group Basis of Politics: A Study in Basing-Point Legislation* (Ithaca: Cornell University Press, Amherst College, 1952), chap. 1, "Group Conflict and the Political Process," pp. 1–53; and David B. Truman, *The Governmental Process: Political Interests and Public Opinion*, A Borzoi Book (New York: Alfred A. Knopf, 1958). Some of the better-known applications of the theory to American politics include Stephen Kemp Bailey, *Congress Makes a Law: The Story Behind the Employment Act of 1946* (New York: Columbia University Press, 1950); Galbraith, *American Capitalism*; Oliver Garceau, *The Political Life of the American Medical Association* (Hamden, Conn.: Archon Books, 1961); Bertram M. Gross, *The Legislative Struggle: A Study in Social Combat*, McGraw-Hill Series in Political Science, ed. by Joseph P. Harris (New York: McGraw-Hill Book Co., 1953); Pendleton Herring, *Group Representation Before Congress*, Institute for Government Research: Studies in Administration (New York: Russell and Russell, Antheneum House, 1967); Latham, *Group Basis of Politics*, pp. 54–227; Arthur Maass, *Muddy Waters: The Army Engineers and the Nation's Rivers,* with a foreword by Harold L. Ickes, Harvard Political Studies (Cambridge: Harvard University Press, 1951); and E. E. Schattschneider, *Party Government* (New York: Rinehart and Co., Publishers, 1942).

6. Truman, *Governmental Process*, "overlapping group membership," p. x, and "Cohesion and Overlapping Membership," pp. 157–67 and passim, in Part 2, "Group Organization and Problems of Leadership," pp. 109–210.

7. Ibid., "the democratic mold," pp.129–39 and passim, in Part 2, "Group Organization and Problems of Leadership," pp. 109–210, "democratic" quoted for clarification in first usage and "democratic mold" quoted in occasional instances.

8. For an unusually direct statement of the dependence of the theory of pluralism in the United States on the doctrine of the free market, cf., Galbraith, *American Capitalism*.

9. Cf., Currin V. Shields, "The American Tradition of Empirical Collectivism," *The American Political Science Review*, March 1952, pp. 104–20.

10. In fact, pluralists commonly freeze "reality" into a model that cannot allow for any kind of systemic transition. Then the model is applauded as a theory, even though models are not theories. In this manner most contemporary advocates of pluralism have effectively slipped the gap from "ought" to "is" and are propounding a doctrine based on an a-priori-deductive methodology rooted in the doctrine of the free market. Many, of course, would prefer the term "normative theory," an oxymoronic attempt to burnish their scientific credentials through a "theory" which is not a theory—because it expresses no interest in trying to explain the existence of what appears to be reality—but which is actually a doctrinal claim about what reality should be.

11. Cf., "active minority," Garceau, *Political Life of the American Medical Association*, p. 18 and passim, and, more generally, chap. 2, "Political Histology: the 'active minority,'" pp. 30–67, quoted for emphasis in its first usage and occasionally throughout; and, Truman, *Governmental Process*, "The Active Minority," pp. 139–55 and passim, in Part 2, "Group Organization and Problems of Leadership," pp. 109–210.

12. James Madison, *Federalist*, no. 10, pp. 53–62, and, in particular, pp. 53–55.

13. For a substantial list of such variations on "democracy," cf., Bertram Gross, *Friendly Fascism: The New Face of Power in America* (New York: M. Evans and Co., 1980), pp. 351–54.

14. Cf., Alan D. Beyerchen, *Scientists Under Hitler: Politics and the Physics Community in the Third Reich* (New Haven: Yale University Press, 1977).

15. As, for instance, in Galbraith, *New Industrial State*, chap. 2, "The Imperatives of Technology," pp. 11–21 and passim.

16. Sir Ernest Barker, "Reflections on English Political Theory," *Political Studies: The Journal of the Political Studies Association of the United Kingdom* (Oxford: Oxford University Press, at the Clarendon Press, February, 1953), p. 8 and passim.

17. Cf., "warranted assertability," John Dewey, *Logic: The Theory of Inquiry* (New York: Henry Holt and Co., 1938), p. 9 and passim, quoted for emphasis in its first usage.

18. Robert Michels, *Political Parties: A Sociological Study of the Oligarchical Tendencies of Modern Democracy*, with an intro. by Seymour Martin Lipset, Trans. by Eden and Cedar Paul (New Brunswick: Transaction Publishers, 1999), and, in particular, Part 6, "Synthesis: The Oligarichal Tendencies of Organization," pp. 331–71, especially chap. 2, "Democracy and the Iron Law of Oligarchy," pp. 342–56 and passim. Also cf., "Author's Preface" to the 1915 edition, pp. 5–7. especially pp. 6 and 7.

19. Michael Polanyi, 4, "The Republic of Science: Its Political and Economic Theory, 1962," pp. 49–72, in Michael Polanyi, *Knowing and Being: Essays by Michael Polanyi*, ed. with an intro. by Marjorie Grene, in Part 2, "The Nature of Science," pp. 47–120 (Chicago: University of Chicago Press, 1969), p. 55.

20. Leslie A. White, *The Science of Culture: A Study of Man and Civilization* (New York: Farrar, Straus, and Co., 1949), chap. 1, "Science is Sciencing," pp. 3–21 and passim. Thus science is not a compilation of verified knowledge; it is the search for what is not yet verified, or in any way known or even thought about. That is, science is not a noun. It is a verb.

21. Walter Lippmann, *Drift and Mastery: An Attempt to Diagnose the Current Unrest*, with a rev. intro. and notes by William E. Leuchtenburg (Madison: The University of Wisconsin Press, 1985), p. 151.

Chapter Ten

From Liberal Man to Democratic Man

For the human psyche to have no effect on the world beyond itself—to not matter in this regard—is intolerable. Of course, there are many ways to try to matter and some are destructive and some supportive of the more egalitarian predilections within people in general. Either way, however, they ultimately express a need for power. Those who are most aware of this overtly seek public effect; those who are less aware also seek this, although they are not quite so sure about what it is they seek.

It is true that certain instances of abject poverty do offer evidence of all adult members of a population sharing the authority of civic decision in a rather equal manner. But these are invariably small-scale communities most of which dramatically changed with the invention of the idea of the private ownership of productive property: a development that slowly allowed people to escape a pervasive scarcity through a greater technological efficiency that led to surpluses and social-class and elite systems of ever-larger jurisdictions. Still, the intention of democracy is to move beyond all this. The intellectual and material promise of the radical Enlightenment is inextricably related to a search for political equality within a world of at least a moderate degree of affluence.

The study of economics has largely been a search for more production at greater efficiencies. But the democratic outlook must finally become free of this preoccupation because it represents an approach to politics which only abundance will allow. Indeed, the denser issues of democracy revolve around the psychological basis of human actualization which may ramify into the maximization of freedom as this is inherently fused with an escape from material necessity and, concurrently, the emerging effect of expressive labor. What is thus propounded is a theory of historical motion that presumably never stops since the clash of tradition with what may be achievable endlessly induces tensions within people as well as among them. Herein resides the prime purpose of the democratic perspective—a search for an increasing array of individual valences that radiate from the nexus of an equality of power—a combination which composes the conclusive content of freedom as the democrat comprehends it.

* * *

Majority rule would seem to follow. Nevertheless, the authority of the majority can be achieved in a manner that encourages the more retrograde and authoritarian tendencies of the species—a possibility that inescapably lurks within the doctrine of democracy. Thus to espouse the democratic position is to confront the actuality that "we are the most constructive and the most destructive of all species, we imagine and dream, hope and fear as no other"[1]; that there are contradictory dispositions within human nature; that these seek both oppression and freedom; and that the paramount commitments of a political system will suppress or encourage each in varying proportions.

Liberalism historically avoids these complexities by simplifying them into an endless quest for wealth accumulation. People are defined by the laws of the market and a fixed economic nature which insists that human beings are not only what they are, but what they always have been and will be. In the liberal view, any denial of these fundamental truths must eventuate in a tyranny wherein communal power will overwhelm the authentic propensities of the possessive individual.[2] The private integrity of economic man can only be threatened and deranged by the undue authority of the public realm.

As a consequence, liberals attempt to escape history by denying the essential role of culture in the shaping of what people are and what they might become. All is circumscribed by the social contract and its self-evident basis in human nature. What is dynamic is the market, and a competitive struggle for material wealth accordingly becomes the most sublime motivation of man—a truth which must lead to the "rational" understanding of what it means to be civilized. Such a cramped and frozen conception of the generic traits of human beings is the true meaning of "the end of ideology"[3] or, more recently, "the end of history"[4]—the de facto proclamation of any successful movement that has exhausted the logic of its controlling formulations.

* * *

In contrast to this, democracy finds its raison d'être in the furtherance of the more generous inclinations within the species: a difficult proposition about process and progress wherein the democrat perceives each personality as a typically fluid and even unpredictable derivation of culture and history. Although their positive potentialities are innate, the functional realities of human behavior are shaped by the phenomenon of development—or more accurately, for those who adhere to the radical Enlightenment, by a teleologi-cal emergence—that is supported by certain kinds of communities and re-tarded by others. Involved here is an essential debate about the impact of nature and nurture wherein the radical version of the Enlightenment contends that human fulfillment is based on real citizenship, and that this demands an active and equal immersion in the polis. In its absence, moving toward this condition becomes fundamental.

Such, of course, is a formulation that the Fascists and Nazis also purport to adopt. However, aside from ignoring the impossibility of a large system being democratic, they transform the polis into the life of the organic nation that assimilates the person into the mission of the state—thereby rendering the word totalitarian anathema to a liberal consciousness which, it might be noted, conveniently fails to apply its own critique to a commercial corpora-tism that would also civilize the world. And, if fascism and Nazism empha-size the necessity of sameness, so does the liberal construction of economic man. It is only the democrat who presses for that crucial variation which must emerge from the equality inherent in unalienated labor and the civic participation of everyone as an equal yet unique individual. This could yield anarchy or, for those who perceive the necessity of government, a system of majority rule. But, within a condition of gesellschaft, its more likely outcome is an increasingly egalitarian pluralism in regard to the power to affect public decisions.

* * *

As Hannah Arendt suggests, once economic necessity is surpassed people have been traditionally driven by a desire for either wealth or fame. In a liberal order these fuse into an esteem for material acquisition which, in turn, yields the entitlement, privilege, and psychological authority which fame yields and that results in power over others. This is an outlook that is usually framed in the lexicon of free markets. Nonetheless, in face of a growing societal affluence, the focus of those who manage big business now becomes less directed to the bottom line per se and more overtly attentive to the attainment of societal power because they know, at least implicitly, that when entitlement, privilege, and psychological authority are widely distrib-uted their influence begins to dissolve.

Of course, material scarcity is fundamental to human history. It is there-fore not surprising that people confronted by a level of affluence previously unknown will admire consumption and act accordingly—perhaps an expres-sion of an insatiable passion for wealth or, conceivably, a period of develop-mental immaturity in the face of a new reality. Indeed it is frequently pro-pounded, especially by many on the "Left," that when incomes are not made the subject of public debate people will be diverted by matters which are far less vital than those which truly affect their existence. Quite often this is portrayed as a situation wherein the voters do not know their own interests. Typically attributed to the vacuous and even insidious quality of the mass media, the result is a lack of awareness that some contend can be reversed only by allowing wealth distributions to become far less equitable than they already are. There are even those who favor economic depressions to wake people up.

However, the facts are more complicated and, from a democratic point of view, may be more encouraging. Contrary to reflexive liberal absolutes about economic man and the meaning of opportunity and interests, it might not take a very high level of material expectation for human beings to become preoccupied with other versions of each. These then become their interests—a reality that is already the case for most who actively engage in politics—and who generally perceive the public good to be a more pressing matter than the maximization of their own monetary gain.

With an enhanced expectation of affluence, such behavior is now replicated in increasingly widespread demands for greater personal gratification, affirmation, and meaning—a manifestation of the easier availability of leisure which permits these needs to more overtly seek outward articulation. As a result, the empirically discernible momentum of more people toward civic involvement becomes evident—a phenomenon which pluralizes the notion of interest and that expresses the classical democratic idea of opportunity as a desire for effect in the polis.

It is in these terms that the democratic notion of progress resonates as an abiding American concern. Despite the fact that the habits of avarice and elitism are stubborn, tensions about values become more palpable as advanced technology causes an actual scarcity to recede. These attain increasingly diverse manifestations as those deeper needs released by even a glimpse of abundance more persistently demand to be heard. From a democratic point of view, they begin to reflect the possibility that a generalized material affluence is reachable; that this is where animal history ends and human history begins—a process that commences with diminishing marginal utility well before the problem of scarcity is literally solved. Or, as Sidney Hook cogently puts it in reference to Marx's portrait of the dilemmas that infuse human development following the dissolution of social-class systems, "man . . . moves from the plane of the pitiful to the plane of the tragic."[5] Herein articulated is the essential democratic outlook about the evolution of the species—a journey that moves away from the stultifying constrictions of economic man toward the more subtle and paradoxical difficulties of political man.

This is a proposition which is well illustrated by Walter Goldschmidt, who depicts the most profound aspirations of people as a "need for positive affect,"[6] a need, he argues, that the empirical evidence suggests is a motivation found within every culture and among the entire range of the discrete personalities that compose them. It is a finding that centrally accords with the democratic position, which further contends that for this need to be at all fulfilled civic power must become more equally distributed. The conjecture of Hegel that humanity dialectically moves from a condition wherein one is free, to a condition in which a few are free, then to a condition wherein the many are free and, finally, to a condition in which all are free begins to emerge as relevant and essential. This is much more than the idea of individual liberty, or rights, as an arena wherein the authority of the state cannot reach, but of freedom as the power to transform the world. Plainly required is a far more egalitarian configuration of political authority than any which human beings in general have come close to achieving: a world wherein freedom is comprehended as inseparable from the public effect of the positive productive powers of everyone.

The influence of this on Marx is evident. Still, as a "Young Hegelian," and a devotee of Ludwig Feuerbach, he wants to "stand Hegel on his feet"[7] by maintaining that freedom does not result from ideas but, on the contrary, that the very idea of freedom is a consequence of the material realities of societal existence. Yet, discarding the traditional approach of great-man history as the story of heroic figures in favor of what will become known as social history—an early version of quantum forecasting[8] about the probable behavior of populations which both Hegel and Marx apply to the transitions of social stages—both affirm that until all are free no one is truly free since the freedom of those who rule is constricted and distorted by the necessity of employing power over others, and because the energy expended to protect a system of "power over" drains any instance of "the power to"[9] of much, if not the totality, of its positive content. For the democrat, freedom, in its fullest sense, mandates that publicly effective power must finally be held by each in an equal manner because this is the only political arrangement that allows people to begin to actualize the outward expression of their more human qualities. Here is the essence of the radical Enlightenment—a perspective that involves an emphasis on process, not form, and that cannot exceed the general level of material wealth and its manifestation in a release from financial concerns which allows real democratic progress to occur.

What this suggests is that immediate economic realities are always pivotal to any tendency toward the emergence of political man.[10] And among the currently most cogent of these are the political implications of affluence.[11] There is no doubt that corporate concentration is more efficient than free markets in the provision of goods and services—at least in reference to those that lend themselves to the techniques of mass production—and it is precisely the corporate impulse that already has led a small part of the planet away from abject material necessity and into a substantial alleviation of scarcity.[12] Yet, to the liberal mind, any chance to actually end scarcity is beyond reach due to the intrinsically avaricious nature of man. Indeed, that poverty still exists in the United States is more a tribute to this largely unassailable conviction—along with its definition of the appropriate distribution of the wealth—than it is to the productive capacities of the order. Nevertheless, in the face of an incessant barrage of official applause for market values, even a glimpse of affluence releases a human yearning for free or unalienated labor as a concrete and public expression of power and a vital ingredient of dignity and self-actualization[13]—a yearning that persistently becomes more widespread and apparent.

* * *

Hence democracy is an argument which must affirm that private behavior incessantly seeks effect beyond itself and that individual actions are invariably suffused with a public content. Stubbornly refusing to perceive the essential pluralism within majorities, it is exactly this which motivates those who resist what they view as the tyrannical proclivities of the many—especially as they may disturb the individual right to productive property. In the United States this is an outlook which is rooted in the rational elitism that infuses the great liberal formulations of constitutionalism and capitalism. And, of course, as with any expression of the Enlightenment, the rational, the true, and the moral cohere because they are each other.

Still, whatever its philosophical foundation, this is an outlook that depends on an elitist or, at least, an elite assertion about the political inequality of human beings. Indeed, special claims to govern are almost always rooted in the assumption that only certain people are endowed with an innately superior capacity to comprehend a preexisting body of knowledge required for right rule. Often mistaken for it, this far exceeds mere snobbery; it is, instead, elitism, a deeply held conviction based on absolute certainties about the naturally unequal qualities among human beings. Whether, depending on the subsequent claim, these qualities need to be developed or not, such an assumption about the qualified one, or few, or even a majority is the necessary seedbed of all elitist doctrines. Hence it must assume that the information, or knowledge or, ultimately, the wisdom required to govern can only be possessed, in part or in full, by a superior few—or, perhaps, by one or the many—but not by all. It thereby denies the egalitarian conviction that if people are not equally rational and, consequently, moral in their presently operative abilities, they are so in their inherent capacities—the unavoidable core of the democratic argument.

The exception to this historically pervasive view about the natural source of leadership is the lesser contention that it is not human nature, but particular kinds of education, training, or experience, or a stipulated combination of any of these, that produces those who compose the appropriate elite, or elites. This usually leads to an argument for government by experts who are wholly the result of a proper environment: a variation of elite rule that is not truly elitist since it does not depend on the contention that a particular person—or persons—uniquely possess an inborn capacity for the making of correct public decisions.

As material plenitude increases and the opportunities for civic influence expand to more people, these are matters that go beyond semantics and the question of who is truly democratic. Certainly, they disclose that those who most vociferously applaud democracy most often want to avoid it. More usefully, however they help to illuminate the salient differences among the democratic argument for a greater equality of power; the wary liberal preference for government by competing commercial elites; and the absolutist elitism of the conservative outlook. In so doing, they work to clarify what the proponents of these very different traditions are actually saying about the inescapable issues of human nature and who should rule.

To be sure, it is frequently maintained that doctrinal disputes of this kind are irrelevant: that the practical reality is that every order is governed by some combination of competing or circulating elites—a pluralistic analysis generally adhered to by many scholars of politics. One way or another, within the domain of contemporary theory such a conclusion usually is a variation on what Gaetano Mosca depicts as the political formula. And among the available choices, as Mosca tellingly declares, the democratic formula is the most stable because it encourages a system of elite rule wherein majorities cannot really complain about policy outcomes since they believe they actually govern, and that public policies are somehow articulations of their own will.[14]

Plainly, to convince others—and oneself—that an order is democratic when it is not, effectively protects the power of those who possess it. This is an approach that becomes increasingly common during the modern era wherein democracy is the alleged goal of nearly everyone. It also disguises the pervading importance of culture, of those dominant perceptions about the propriety of established power configurations that induce a general willingness to identify with and even serve the prevailing interests within a society—an inclination which is patently indispensable for admission into any of the influential social classes and established elites that actually define the order. Thus "today . . . it is official doctrine among industrial democracies that a political society is to be judged as certifiably democratic if it has free political parties and free elections."[15] In the West this is usually articulated as liberal democracy, a formula that precisely promotes the continuity of government by competing propertied elites against the threat of popular and, especially, working-class discontent.

Moreover, the composition of any majority is likely to fluctuate according to the issues being confronted and the intensity of various interests regarding them and, over any period of time, and what will probably emerge is an acceptable range of shifting majorities. Certainly Jefferson's proposal for continuing majorities implies a substantial measure of volatility and even instability. However, corporate liberals may have little need to worry. As noted by some who laud democracy as the most stable and even conservative of orders, while majorities may vary in reference to specific concerns, they will usually manifest a reflexive acceptance of the economic arrangements to which they are conditioned—along with the cultural mandates which articulate and support these arrangements. They will be moderate, or centrist. That is, majorities will typically adapt to the controlling ideas of those who wield societal power.

Nevertheless, the goal of the radical Enlightenment is not systemic quietude; it is the end of elite rule. And to be a democrat is to focus on the connections between the transformative process of people struggling to become what they might be and the material milieu within which these struggles take place. As a consequence, it is a perspective which accords with scientific understandings about the difficulties that attend species development and the probabilities of more profound levels of human "imagination, sensibility and intellect"[16] being actualized within a condition where all positive talents are equally appreciated. It follows that its emphasis is always on those needs for assertion, affirmation, and dignity that accompany personality integration—needs that, for most people, are yet to attain a meaningful, consistent, and observable ability to influence the larger world. However, unlike biological evolution, the pattern of this motion is not conceived of as random. Instead, the democratic outlook projects a progressive fulfillment of those deeper and more redeeming propensities of the psyche which are integral to human nature but which historically have been held to have little chance of aggregate realization, even while concurrently insisting that such realization must be grounded in the actualities of history itself.

This centrally involves those perceptions, values, and attitudes which compose a culture and, finally, a society—along with the depth and inclusiveness of what Erich Fromm refers to as the social unconscious through which they are expressed.[17] Such considerations are critical to a doctrine that anticipates the arrival of a world wherein a traditional preoccupation with material survival will rationally give way to the expectation of a decent level of financial well-being—an expectation that will release a universal need for power that is simultaneously public and personal. It is why, in the final analysis, the principle of majority rule cannot be separated from the transformative issue of the substance of an aggregate consciousness about the ingredients of power within a material history—an issue which elevates the democratic argument about political man into a meaningful contribution to political thought.

* * *

Of course, when, and if, this leads to a more egalitarian system of civic power the result may well be a stultifying conformity. But the democrat is finally betting that people in general are rational and empirical. Accordingly, when they can, they will move from a preoccupation with eating to a concern with their more positive and complex individual identities and to a yearning to express these identities through freedom as power in labor and polis. It is this which Marx portrays as the beginning of species man fleeing the cocoon of animal man [18] in a search for an interior telos which is distributed by nature in a manner wherein the uniqueness of each is of benefit to all—a profoundly pluralizing process that mandates an escape from the elitism, deprivation, exploitation, and contortion of self that infuse social-class struggles and epitomize "the muck of ages." [19]

That a development of this magnitude would constitute a central challenge to the preeminent liberal idea of human nature is evident. After all, what might evolve is a more universal equality of treatment or, more disturbingly, a greater equality of material condition or result for the undeserving. At least it so appears to those who are currently cloaked with authority and who now often find themselves confronted by demands they reflexively, if often unconsciously, abhor—and that they frequently fail to comprehend because, at bottom, these demands are less about money, or property rights, or even rights in general, than they are about the far more complicated human need for power. [20] That is, they are about the emergence of political man as an expression of the material foundations of a more egalitarian pluralism.

All of this infers an elevated notion of the political. If, as John C. Calhoun correctly notes, force and coercion represent the breakdown of politics, the democratic proposal is for the political in its fundamental and most noble sense of civic engagement. [21] Within such a conception, there is a rightness to power as instrumental to the civilizing influence of freedom. It is in this context, once released from the prison of economic concerns, that the increasingly positive motivations of human beings will begin to transcend the more well-known theories of Marx and creep toward those of Freud—although hints of Freud are clearly to be found in the work of Marx, most systematically in his earlier writings.

Both liberals and conservatives, despite their own claims that they represent the will of the people, apprehend this prospect with dread—precisely as did the Fascists and the Nazis. This cannot be surprising. A greater equality of public action is always the bête noire that any elitist position, consciously or otherwise, must repel or, at a minimum, impede. Perceiving exactly this, and under a magnified egalitarian pressure, many liberals begin to adopt a more authoritarian stance. Yet this is also nothing new. Liberals have long been quick to trim other civil liberties when the property system, upon which all liberty is presumably predicated, is considered to be under assault. To avoid the supposed downward leveling and oppression of the popular passions of the moment, some even gravitate toward the oppression of a police state as an unfortunate price of stability. Without a doubt, the emergence of political man contains tyrannical possibilities. But then, so does economic man. The larger effects of affluence are not a guarantee of freedom. For the radical Enlightenment, however, they are a necessary condition.

NOTES

1. Douglas Dowd, *U.S. Capitalist Development Since 1776: Of, By, and For Which People?* (Armonk, NY: M. E. Sharpe, 1993), p. 80.

2. Cf., Macpherson, *Political Theory of Possessive Individualism*, p. v and passim, cited supra, chap. 1, n. 3, and chap. 9, n. 4.

3. Bell, *End of Ideology*, pp. 39–47, cited supra, chap. 1, n. 8, and chap. 2, n. 3.

4. Fukuyama, *End of History,* and Fukuyama, "End of History?," *National Interest*, Summer 1989, pp. 3–18, cited supra, chap. 1, n. 9, and chap. 2, n. 3.

5. Sidney Hook, *Towards the Understanding of Karl Marx: A Revolutionary Interpretation* (New York: The John Day Co., 1933), p. 101.

6. Walter Goldschmidt, *Man's Way: A Preface to the Understanding of Human Society* (New York: Holt, Rinehart and Winston, A Holt-Dryden Book, 1959), "The Need for Positive Affect," pp. 26–30, in chap. 1, "The Biological Constant," pp. 17–30 and passim, italicized for emphasis in the first usage.

7. Such as in Marx, "Economic and Philosophic Manuscripts of 1844," in Tucker (ed.), *Marx-Engels Reader*, p. 112 and passim, cited supra, chap. 9, n. 7.

8. Cf., Heilbroner, *Future as History,* chap. 1, "Encounter with History," pp. 11–58, and, in particular, pp. 28–30, cited supra, chap. 8, no. 3.

9. Cf., Fromm, *Anatomy of Human Destructiveness*, pp. 235–67 and passim, and Fromm, *Man for Himself*, p. 88 and passim, both cited supra, chap. 10, n. 10.

10. There are, of course, other views regarding this possibility. Among the more intriguing is that articulated in Hans J. Morgenthau, *Scientific Man vs. Power Politics* (Chicago: The University of Chicago Press, Phoenix Books, 1974). For a more typical "realist" approach to this issue, cf., Seymour Martin Lipset, *Political Man: The Social Bases of Politics*, expanded edition (Baltimore: The Johns Hopkins University Press, 1981).

11. Cf., Galbraith, *Affluent Society.* Also of interest is James P. Young, *The Politics of Affluence: Ideology in the United States Since World War II*, Chandler Publications in Political Science, ed. by Victor Jones (San Francisco: Chandler Publishing Co., 1968), and, in particular, p. 214 and passim. A conservative reaction to this reality can be found in Samuel P. Huntington, chap. 3, "The United States," in Michael Crozier, Samuel P. Huntington, and Joji Watanuki, *The Crisis of Democracy: Report on the Governability of Democracies to the Trilateral Commission* (New York: New York University Press, 1975), pp. 59–118, and, especially, p. 63. Not surprisingly, Huntington insists that "the effective operation of a democratic political system usually requires some measure of apathy and noninvolvement on the part of some individuals and groups," ibid., p. 114, a strange understanding of "democratic" which is, nonetheless, extremely popular in contemporary liberal systems, usually in the guise of "constitutional democracy," p. 63 and passim. Also note section IV, "The Democratic Distemper: Consequences," pp. 102–6, and section V, "The Democratic Distemper: Causes," pp. 106–13 and passim. This is concurrently labeled a "democratic surge" ibid., p. 60, and "an excess of democracy," p. 113.

12. For a concise statement of these dynamics, cf., Galbraith, *New Industrial State*, and, most specifically, chap. 2, "The Imperatives of Technology," pp. 11–21, chap. 3, "The Nature of Industrial Planning," pp. 22–34, and chap. 4, "Planning and the Supply of Capital," pp. 35–45.

13. Cf., A. H. Maslow, 7, "A Theory of Human Motivation," pp. 153–73, and 8, "Self-Actualizing People: A Study of Psychological Health," in *Dominance, Self-Esteem, Self-Actu-*

alization: Germinal Papers of A. H. Maslow, ed. by Richard S. Lowry, International Study Project (Monterey, CA: Brooks/Cole Publishing Co., 1973), pp. 177–201, and, in particular, p. 162 and passim, italicized in first usage as a section heading. Maslow attributes the term, "self-actualization," ibid., p. 163, to Kurt Goldstein, *The Organism: A Holistic Approach to Biology Derived from Pathological Data in Man*, with a foreword by K. S. Lashley, American Psychology Series, ed. by Henry E. Garrett (New York: American Book Co., 1939), p. 194 and passim, capitalized in subtitle, pp. 197 and 203, no hyphen, p. 326, and, italicized for emphasis, pp. 197 and 446.

14. Gaetano Mosca, *The Ruling Class: Elementi di Scienza Politica*, ed. and rev., with an intro. by Arthur Livingston, trans. by Hannah D. Kahn (New York: McGraw-Hill Book Co., 1939), p. 70 and passim, quoted for emphasis in the original in its first usage, through which, in one or another of its several variations, all systems are allegedly governed. Especially relevant is the contention that in allegedly democratic orders "the leaders of the governing class are the exclusive interpreters . . . of the will of the people . . . and when no other organized social forces exist apart from those which represent the principle on which sovereignty is based . . . there can be no resistance, no effective control, to restrain a natural tendency in those who stand at the head of the social order to abuse their powers," ibid., p. 134. This, of course, is a classical liberal perception of the necessary consequences of any egalitarian claim, a claim which must result in "an organized minority prevailing over a disorganized majority," ibid., p. 146.

15. Wolin, *Tocqueville Between Two Worlds*, p. 253.

16. Henry King Stanford, chap. 11, "How Humanizing Are the Humanities?," pp. 189–204, in Henry King Stanford, *Campus Under Political Fire and Other Essays* (n. p.: n. d.), p. 190.

17. Cf., Erich Fromm, *Beyond the Chains of Illusion: My Encounter with Marx and Freud* (New York: Simon & Schuster, A Trident Press Book, 1962), chap. 9, "The Social Unconscious," pp. 88–134, and, in particular, "social unconscious," p. 88 and passim, quoted occasionally for emphasis in its early usage.

18. As, for instance, in Marx, "Economic and Philosophical Manuscripts in Tucker (ed.), *Marx-Engels Reader*, 2nd ed., pp. 115–17.

19. Marx, *German Ideology*, ibid., p. 193.

20. Again, in a perverse manner, Huntington, chap. 3, "The United States," in Crozier, Huntington, and Watanuki, *Crises of Democracy*, pp. 15–118.

21. Calhoun, "Disquisition on Government," p. 1 and passim, cited supra, chap. 6, n. 17.

Conclusion

Science and Democracy

On its face, democracy is not a theory about who actually wields authority, and why, and how. It is, instead, a doctrinal construction about who should possess authority, and why, and for what purposes it ought to be exercised. And, as with any doctrine, all of this must be grounded in a priori presuppositions and assumptions about the nature of the universe, society, and man.

But doctrines can also flow from a search for the realities of the human experience—that is, from empirical support of hypotheses and theories—which, to be sure, is itself dependent on presuppositions and assumptions about the nature of evidence—as well as on the observations that may verify or falsify these hypotheses and theories. Accordingly, a political doctrine can emerge from a consensus about the findings of a scientific investigation into the societal proclivities of human beings.

In this sense democracy, as a political expression of the radical Enlightenment, is more deeply suggestive than its commitment to political equality and majority rule, or even to its affection for popular sovereignty and an insistence on the consent of the governed. A serious democratic claim has to move beyond the formalities of doctrinal principles and attempt to comprehend the nuanced complexities of the needs and desires of vast aggregates of people.

At a fundamental level, these are matters which reflect the organizational imperatives of the prevailing means and mode of production. Thus the human desire for greater economic efficiency caused a global transition from what Karl Marx and Frederick Engels suggest was a primitive communism to a variety of social-class systems rooted in notions of the ownership and control of productive property.[1] Moreover, the behavior of the elites within each class became central to maintaining particular systems, even while the greater material abundance which followed led to changing conceptions of opportunity. One consequence of this are demands for an ever-greater expansion of the idea of equality, not only of rights, but also of power—a phenomenon which, for many in America, now emerges as a disturbing reality.

However, such is a process that never moves in a linear pattern. On the contrary, it is expressed in the spiraling configurations of a dialectical history characterized by contradiction and punctuated by episodic surges of progressive achievement. And it is predictably accompanied by those reactions that urgently seek to reestablish a status-quo ante while never quite succeeding. This always involves how the aggregate consciousness of a population defines interests, an issue which invariably reveals a view of the human possibilities, along with formulations about the proper extent, substance, and allocation of societal power and political authority.

* * *

"The philosophers have only *interpreted* the world, in various ways; the point, however, is to change it."[2] This comprises the necessary context of any call for self-government. But such a call plainly does not end with the matter of who holds the offices of government, even if they are in the hands of majorities. And it is more than a negative proposal for the end of a long history of minority rule. At bottom, democracy is rooted in the conviction that any special claim to the knowledge purportedly required for right rule must be subject to reason and, finally, the publicly verifiable or falsifiable test of empirical evidence: a conviction that is of greater political significance than an actual implementation of majority rule. This is because authority, in both its political and psychological senses, can only derive from a successful assertion of the knowledge necessary to govern, and because this purported knowledge is ultimately controlled by agreements about the methodology through which it is attained.

In this regard, the compatibility of the scientific conception of knowledge as process and a democratic reliance on continuing majorities[3] is significant. Science and democracy are necessarily linked because the expansion of reason and empiricism are central to the democratic worldview, and because it is only from the disruptions of consciousness which science historically induces that any serious furtherance of democracy can commence. This involves methodological values that finally include everyone in the process of confirmation. It leads to a version of the polis which insists that to not be actively involved in the public life is not to be engaged in a fully human existence. Moreover, any argument for democracy based on feeling becomes an oxymoron since it is exactly the aspirations of reason as expressed through the procedures of science that allow the development of a cultural outlook which complies with the fundamental content of the democratic perspective.

The problem with democracy is not human nature, but the systemic realities wherein people must function. Rooted in the premise that everyone must have full and equal access to the relevant facts, the radical Enlightenment places confidence in the equal capacity of each to act in a reasonable and, accordingly, moral manner on the basis of the information available to them. This becomes a minimal democratic commitment. Yet there is a problem with this. Clearly, de facto jurisdictions of extensive geographic size that come to surpass even the reach of nation-states; huge numbers of people typically too removed from what is going on to even associate particular public officials with specific policies, or even with the effects of these policies on their own lives; and an order driven by the obscure global interconnectedness of industrial and postindustrial economies concurrently define and disguise the factual situation.

Additionally, there is little evidence for the tangential proposition that if so-far unprovable differences in rational capacity do happen to actually exist and, since there are probably different kinds of rationality, or intelligence, in the first place, the chances of reasonable action by a majority are statistically better than political decisions which are left to one or a few. Beyond this, to rely on popular sovereignty is patently useless when it comes to the question of who should rule except to say by all; to merely focus on a more equitable distribution of the wealth is not adequate unless this is what the majority commands; and, finally, the substitution of representative government for the reality of self-government is never a democratic position. Whatever human nature may be, these are realities within which people must function. They lead, however, not to democracy but to a condition of mass politics, wherein any sensible egalitarian argument can have little to do with the necessary localism of majority government.

* * *

As Jefferson anticipated, the democrat needs to forgo the stipulations of a literal democracy and establish a fall-back position. Most centrally, those who would seriously promote democracy or, at least, the potentialities of a more egalitarian politics in a postindustrial age, need to discover democratic tendencies in a world where the economic foundation of the ward-republic—or any of its functional equivalencies—no longer exists. In short, another material basis for a greater equality of civic power must be found. This has to encourage an expanding pluralism of public influence in a manner which addresses the forces of modernity while offering an escape from a consciousness induced by the suzerainty of corporate wealth. It must realize that democracy cannot be about competitive-party elections grounded in a market culture, an arrangement that must eventuate, as it has, in a crypto-polyarchy of consolidated capital with which American democracy is now persistently confused. Finally, it needs to dispute the plutocratic remnants of a capitalist fixation on an endless economic scarcity and its adulation of avarice in the guise of scientific and technological advance.

In a country that, since the Puritan experiment with dynasty, has existed under "the tyrannical force of Lockian sentiment,"[4] and has consequently transformed the political into the economic,[5] it is not surprising that there are very few real conservatives or democrats in America. Still, there are those who accept the conservative idea that there are people qualified to govern unconstrained. And, moving from right to left, there are some who contend that the policies of a complex and global system actually ought to be formulated and implemented by majorities. These arguments also infuse the American ethos, complicating an order dominated by the long economic civil war between laissez-faire liberals and reform liberals and making more opaque the always-pervading issue of power.

It is here that the classical conception of the polis insinuates itself as systemically vital. About this, of course, it is usually claimed that while such aspirations might pertain to certain people, they have no application to most. Thus, for instance, when Hannah Arendt advocates action in the public space as that which makes the inevitable not happen[6]—the citizen in the polis as a crucial manifestation of plurality, contingency, and free will—what is depicted is an opportunity for true civic behavior that, in Arendt's view, should be open to all, but the capacity for which is found in relatively few. These she defines as the "*vitae activa*" people who, by their nature, are of a higher type than those who comprise the multitudes. Among the many, some may have the abilities of "*homo faber*," therein possessing the imagination and skill to create and maintain the artifacts of a world within which human beings can find a home. Then there are the very few, the "*vitae contemplativa*," whose inborn talents finally surpass even those required by the polis because they are capable of the rarified joys of philosophy—a formulation that Plato would avidly applaud. However, in terms of sheer probabilities, people are most likely to be "*animal laborans*" whose only capacity is to endlessly produce for immediate consumption.[7] Accordingly, humanity is rather limited, and a liberal system simply represents a specific version of what Lincoln Steffens declared to be at the core of all politics—an enduring competition, ultimately not for money, but for privilege.[8]

Indeed, where economic necessity is eliminated or, at least, substantially mitigated, a battle for privilege does epitomize human history, even though, to this point, this has been largely played out in terms of authorized entitlements to material largess. Yet, for the democrat, people are capable of far more than this through a transformation in the cultural definition of opportunity from personal wealth to civic action: a transformation that depends on a sufficient diminution of scarcity which will release the energies of humanity into a pivotal confrontation with their own possibilities.

As a semblance of a visible and assumable abundance emerges, a demand for public influence is more overtly expressed by increasing numbers of people who, along with an expanded range of ideas, signify a changing consciousness and its eventual articulation in new ideological commitments. And, contrary to their engrained love of commerce—and a corollary inability to identify the conservative Enlightenment as the source of their discontent—such a development commences with those who evince a growing cynicism about the enormous centralization of economic power which long permeates the content of American policy.

What this suggests is an intrusion of a more pluralistic arrangement of civic effect. Such is a matter which is blatantly public. Still, the advertising genius of a business culture continues, at least so far, to successfully merchandize the private nature of human beings through the assurance that scarcity and alienated labor can never be eliminated; that to be incessantly profit-seeking is to be spontaneous and natural; and that an endless entrepreneurial quest for greater social and personal opulence is nothing other than the major rational activity of the authentic individual.

This outlook often has been encouraged by a reintroduction of financial insecurity as a pervasive reality, including a contrived revival of the intractability of scarcity through the manipulation of industrial, fiscal, and monetary policy. Still, the output of contemporary production is enormous and policies of this kind are difficult to maintain because the manifestations of abundance cannot be effectively hidden for very long. It follows that for a magnifying proportion of the population opportunity as an insatiable passion for more lucre begins to resemble an arcane artifact of a pervasive history of economic necessity which is in the process of dissolution—a development that frequently enhances a sense that we are all in this together and that a broader, more personal, and more egalitarian idea of humanity is required. And, despite the best efforts of those who speak for the barons of big business to induce a fear of scarcity in order to get people in general to worry about money,[9] the dependence of corporate power on the scientific foundation of material plenitude indisputably works against these conditioned inclinations.

So does the increasingly evident fact that a corporate system transfers power away from enterprises which create real wealth through the exploitation of labor to those which manage already-exploited labor in the form of venture capital. Entering the domain of legal abstractions, some are beginning to wonder if corporations are really persons, or if rights actually attach to property itself as distinct from the holders of property. Within a deeply liberal America more people are slowly questioning whether greed is really instinctive; whether opportunity must be rooted in avarice; or even whether the laws of nature actually dictate a right to financially profit from the labor of others especially when, as Edward Bellamy noted quite a while ago, it is plain that whose labor contributed how much to the creation of wealth cannot really be determined.[10] Or, most essentially, whether the qualification to govern should continue to flow from a habitual deference to private claims to a socially produced material surplus.

Hence, as the tangible effects of technological invention continue, the traditional liberal conception of human nature gradually comes to be questioned and increasingly unsettled. This is because, at bottom, the Enlightenment represents the release of organized science as a force of history and an ideological view which becomes the material basis of a more egalitarian pluralism. In this sense, it reflects the struggle of the species to reach its more human potential through free labor and the inherent association of this with a greater equality of public influence. Its raison d'être can be discovered only within the interior tensions that attend this struggle—those major contradictions which transform the substance of society and which are now crucially embedded within the imperatives of scientific technology as a dominant productive reality.

* * *

While this globalizes the reach of power beyond nation-states it simultaneously encourages both an authoritarian corporatism and an expanded idea of the political—a paradox of power which the democrat must understand as a surrogate for the very small jurisdictions that traditionally provide the seedbed of the democratic argument. But what Arendt refers to as the fundamental plurality of human condition[11] is largely opaque to liberal perception because its abiding insistence on the universality and permanence of economic man resists that conviction. Yet the ultimate bulwark against corporatism is not private financial interest but the very public influence of the scientific approach wherein a more egalitarian system of pluralism encourages the emergence of individuality and those pivotal variations among people which articulates this on a large scale. Indeed, any theory of pluralism is really a description of where the dialectics of aspiration and achievement have taken history so far. From the democratic point of view, this is merely a moment in the process of human actualization which is simultaneously personal and public. Accordingly, the more profound issue is not whether democracy is viable for the modern world but how the democratic reflex will next express itself.

Of course, from a liberal perspective, this is perceived to be a fundamental assault on established form by process—a degrading motion seemingly out of control which many liberals have long identified as the presiding anarchy of the modern world. Ideologically conditioned to the negative notions of liberty and rights as differentiated from a positive commitment to freedom and power,[12] the liberal mentality apprehends democrats as making unreasonably naive and often dangerous assumptions about the rational proclivities of most human beings.

And maybe they are. But liberals also rely on many unsupportable formulations to alleviate their anxiety about the tyranny of the many. They admire free markets, and extol rights separate of the issue of the power necessary to their enjoyment, abstractions which are quite detached from any semblance of empirical evidence. Moreover, to the extent that the democratic outlook is vague, this is because it seldom indulges in the detailed projections of a utopian vision, contending that the static quality of a utopia imposes cloture on possibility. It invokes, as it must, a sense of uncertainty, a sense that is compatible with the political volatility of continuing majorities and their integral connection to democracy, as well as to the disturbing dynamics of scientific discovery. And, quite plainly, this is a combination that comprises the conclusive texture of progress.

While a system of mass politics is not democracy, majorities are infused with much more reason, empiricism, and diversity than are the equally habituated responses of the one or the few. They are virtually never typified by absolute agreement—a phenomenon which, when it attains public expression, complies with the understanding that variation is the key to evolutionary success in regard to human societies as well as to the species itself. "Everybody is cleverer than anybody," said Georges Clemenceau. [13] There is much truth to this and, although a majority is not everybody, the chances of adaptive behavior are more likely to ramify from the many than from an elite—or even from a liberal configuration of competing elites. The idea of democracy finally complies with quantum theory in physics by emphasizing the probabilities of variation that attend the aggregate phenomena of the experience of the species.

Within a postindustrial epoch of advanced technology and large jurisdictions, it is this which must inform concerns about unequal financial outcomes while remaining open to a notion of opportunity which promotes an equality of expressive labor and civic power to which people persistently gravitate. It reveals the actuality that democracy is always a force, not a form—a dynamic of emergence that invariably reflects the material conditions of the human situation at any stage in its long crawl toward the individuation that manifests a complex panorama of shared needs and unique personalities. Inseparable from the scientific approach to reality, it is precisely here that the majoritarian position remains vital because of the more profound concerns to which it leads. These slowly become apparent in a new and more human comprehension of opportunity that emphasizes the public as opposed to the private, that distinguishes "power to" from "power over," [14] and that converts the skepticism and openness of science to the positive possibilities of an expanding need for political effect. It is in this manner that the radical Enlightenment becomes the necessary fulfillment of the Enlightenment itself.

NOTES

1. Karl Marx and Frederick Engels, *Manifesto of the Communist Party*, p. 31, cited supra, chap. 6, n.14.

2. Karl Marx, "Theses on Feuerbach," in Tucker (ed.) *Marx-Engels* Reader, pp. 14–15, thesis no. 11, p. 145.

3. Jefferson, "Letter to James Madison," September 6, 1789, in *Papers of Thomas Jefferson*, Boyd (ed.), 20 vols., vol. 15, p. 392 and passim, cited supra, chap. 4, n. 15.

4. Hartz, *Liberal Tradition in America*, p. 31.

5. Wolin, *Politics and Vision*, chap. 9, "Liberalism and the Decline of Political Philosophy," pp. 286–351.

6. Cf., Hannah Arendt, "On Violence," in Hannah Arendt, *Crises of the Republic* (San Diego: Harcourt, Brace and Jovanovich, Publishers, A Harvest, Harcourt Brace and Jovanovich Book, 1969), pp. 132–33.

7. Hannah Arendt, *The Human Condition*, Charles R. Walgreen Foundation Lectures (Chicago: The University of Chicago Press, 1958), pp. 132–33. These types are italicized throughout, presumably for emphasis.

8. In general, in Steffens, *Autobiography of Lincoln Steffens*, cited supra, chap. 8, n. 15.

9. As for instance, in Huntington, chap. 3, "The United States," in Crozier, Huntington, and Watanuki, *Crisis of Democracy*, pp. 59–118, and, especially, 63, cited supra, chap. 10, n. 18.

10. Cf., Edward Bellamy, "What 'Nationalism' Means," *The Contemporary Review*, December 1890, p. 18. Of course, this argument deeply informs the far more famous work, Edward Bellamy, *Looking Backward: 2000–1887*, with an intro. by Robert L. Shurter, The Modern Library (New York: Random House, 1951). For an excellent discussion of this, cf., Claire Goldstene, *The Struggle for America's Promise: Equal Opportunity at the Dawn of Corporate Capital* (Jackson: University Press of Mississippi, 2014), pp. 171–74.

11. Arendt, *Human Condition*, p. 175 and passim.

12. Cf., Berlin, "Two Concepts of Liberty," in Berlin, *Four Essays on Liberty*, pp. 118–72, and, especially, pp. 121–22. Much better is the distinction between "liberty" and "freedom" in Arendt, *On Revolution*, pp. 21–28, 129–30, 135, 220–21, 236–37 and 258–59 and, more generally, chap. 3, "Pursuit of Happiness," pp. 111–37 and passim. Also, cf., Marx and Engels, *Holy Family*, in *Karl Marx, Frederick Engels: Collected Works*, vol. 4, "Marx and Engels: 1844–45," p. 131 and passim, all cited supra, chap. 5, n. 9.

13. Georges Benjamin Clemenceau, as quoted in Carl Sandburg, "The People, Yes," in Carl Sandburg, *Complete Poems: Carl Sandburg*, revised and expanded ed., with an intro. by Archibald Macleish (San Diego: Harcourt Brace and Jovanovich, Publishers, 1970), p. 495.

14. Cf., Fromm, *Anatomy of Human Destructiveness*, pp. 235–67 and passim, and Fromm, *Man for Himself*, p. 88 and passim, both cited supra, chap. 5, n. 10 and chap. 10, n. 9.

Index

About the Author

Paul N. Goldstene received a BA from Wayne State University, taught social studies in public high schools in Detroit and Tucson, and received an MA and PhD in government from the University of Arizona. He taught contemporary political thought and theory at three universities, including, for 32 years, California State University, Sacramento, where he ran the Political Theory Forum for ten years and received the Outstanding Scholarly Achievement Award in 1995. Among his books are *The Collapse of Liberal Empire: Science and Revolution in the Twentieth Century*, Yale University Press (1977), Chandler and Sharp (1980, 2nd ed. 1998); *Democracy in America: Sardonic Speculations: With a Postscript on Equal Opportunity*, Bucknell House (1988); *The Bittersweet Century: Modern Science and American Democracy*, Chandler and Sharp (1989); and *Revolution American Style: The Nineteen-Sixties and Beyond*, Chandler and Sharp (1997). Goldstene has also written numerous articles and book reviews for scholarly publications and was frequently a guest commentator for "Making Contact" on the National Radio Project. He is currently teaching political and constitutional thought for the Osher Lifelong Learning Institute at the University of California, Davis Extension Program.